Dr. Lanni's Orgo 2
Lecture Notebook

Laura Lanni, PhD

LMNOPress

Published by LMNO Press, P.O. Box 544, Chapin, SC 29036

ISBN 978-0-9907757-9-9 (pbk.)

A note from the author

Dear Students,

Organic chemistry is challenging, but once you learn the basics you can apply the concepts over and over in predictable ways. Upon successful completion of two semesters of organic chemistry you'll recognize organic compounds on the labels of foods, beauty products, and household chemicals. You will visualize the strings of atoms that make up polymers like plastic wrap, Styrofoam, PVC pipes, nylons, and polyesters. You'll look up the structures of prescribed medicines and maybe even propose a series of synthetic steps to make them.

I love teaching this course for the broad knowledge base it provides to my students in many future careers. My past students are doctors, nurses or pharmacists who understand drug interactions based on organic chemistry functional groups, and engineers who might design biodegradable plastic or ways to trap and use carbon dioxide from the atmosphere. Understanding organic chemistry leads to many paths. But there is some truth to the old proverb: *You R-O-R' get organic chemistry, or you don't.*

Organic chemistry lectures may feel like a drawing course. Some students report they spend lecture time writing and drawing furiously and they sacrifice listening to do so. This notebook is a lecture shell for my orgo 2 lectures where students can add notes during lecture and devote more time to listening, discussing, and answering questions. I hope my organization of the topics herein helps my students succeed in mastering the material in orgo 2 so (just in case it isn't your favorite course) you can put this behind you and move on with what *you* love.

To my teaching colleagues: you may use my lecture notes at your own peril for your course, especially when you first start teaching. But your best teaching will come from the natural organization of the course material *in your own way* over many years.

Have a good weekend.

Dr. Lanni

First lecture

COURSE SYLLABUS

     Grading (see syllabus)

     Practice Problems (in textbook(s))

     Calendar (lecture outline, recitation quizzes, exams dates)

Course overview and objectives (topics)

START: Review orgo 1, Preview orgo 2

7

Course calendar
on syllabus

Exam dates

Quiz dates

8

e

8

Organometallics, etc

Topics
Carbonyl group
Oxidation (done) and reduction
Reduction of C=O to make alcohol, many reducing reagents
[Oxidation of alcohol to make C=O (or COOH)] (already done in orgo 1)

Organometallics
Prep of organolithium, organomagnesium
Reactions of organometallics
Make alcohols from Grignards (C-C bond formation!)

17

Structure of carbonyl, C=O

Functional groups with C=O
hybridization
Resonance
Polarization
Nucleophilic attack on C=O
(the carbon is electrophilic)

18

Oxidation and reduction

Remember REDOX in general chemistry?

Oxidation and reduction in organic chemistry

Oxidation: oxygen content increases and/or hydrogen content decreases

Reduction: oxygen content decreases and/or hydrogen content increases

Laura Lanni

Oxidation examples by functional group (**Review** from orgo 1)

Alkene → alcohol

Alcohol → aldehyde or ketone

Aldehyde → carboxylic acid or ester

Alkane → alkene → alkyne

More review from orgo 1: Oxidation reagents (for alcohols)(aka oxidizing agents)

H_2CrO_4 (chromic acid), Na_2CrO_4, $H_2Cr_2O_7$, $Na_2Cr_2O_7$

$KMnO_4$

"Jones reagent" $CrO_3/Na_2Cr_2O_7$ in H_2SO_4(aq)

PCC: pyridinium chlorochromate
        Made from CrO_3/HCl in pyridine

HOCl (hypochlorous acid) via NaOCl with acetic acid, 0°C

Oxidation considerations and examples

1° alcohol oxidation

2° alcohol oxidation

cannot oxidize 3° alcohol. Why?

Which reagent to use?

mechanism with HOCl

Oxidation considerations   and examples

1° alcohol oxidation

Oxidation considerations   and examples

2° alcohol oxidation

25

Oxidation considerations   and examples

cannot oxidize 3° alcohol. Why?

26

Oxidation considerations: examples

Which reagent to use?

Oxidation considerations: examples

Ethanol oxidized to ethanal

mechanism with HOCl

Reduction (opposite of oxidation)

Alkyne → alkene → alkane (already know these reactions orgo 1)

Alcohol →Alkene (already know these reactions orgo 1)

aldehyde or ketone → Alcohol

carboxylic acid or ester → Aldehyde (or alcohol)

Some mechanisms

29

Reduction reagents: HYDRIDES

To reduce carbonyl to alcohol use $NaBH_4$ or LAH

Sodium borohydride **$NaBH_4$** vs   Lithium aluminum hydride **$LiAlH_4$** ("LAH")

To reduce ester to aldehyde use DiBAL-H (example)

Also: recall sodium hydride NaH (orgo 1)—a hydride that acts as a strong base

30

Reduction examples

Reduction of C=O → C-OH with $NaBH_4$ or LAH

Ease of reduction of CO functional groups

Which reagent to use?

Examples

Mechanism of hydride attack—for both LAH and $NaBH_4$, the key step is hydride transfer.

Reduction examples

Mechanism of hydride attack—for both LAH and $NaBH_4$, the key step is hydride transfer.

practice

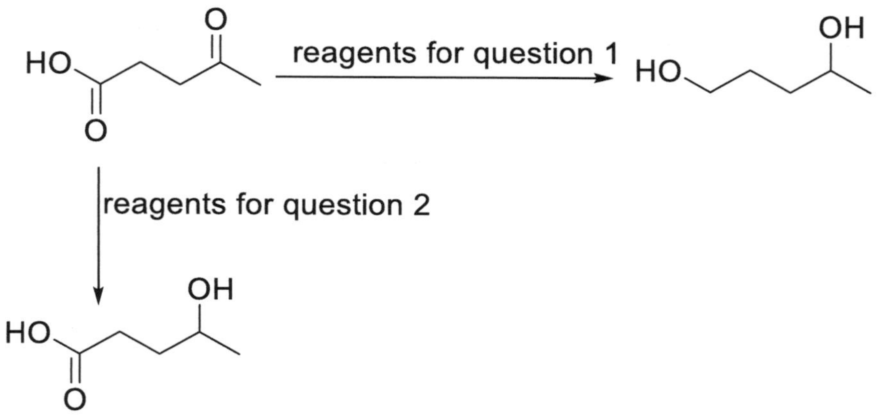

HO
O
O
reagents for question 1
HO
OH
reagents for question 2
HO
OH
O

33

Hydride reductions summary

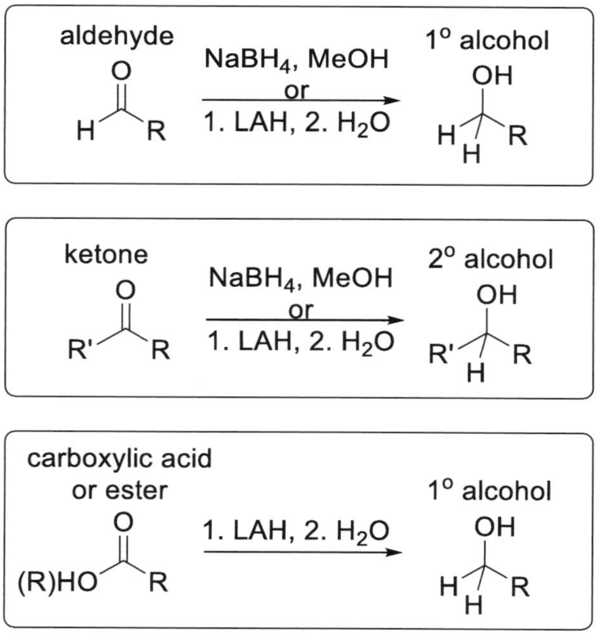

aldehyde
O
H
R
NaBH4, MeOH
or
1. LAH, 2. H2O
1° alcohol
OH
H
H
R
ketone
O
R'
R
NaBH4, MeOH
or
1. LAH, 2. H2O
2° alcohol
OH
R'
H
R
carboxylic acid
or ester
O
(R)HO
R
1. LAH, 2. H2O
1° alcohol
OH
H
H
R

34

Organometallics overview

Carbanion C$^-$ nucleophile!

Reagent preparation (Grignards and organolithiums (and Gilman)

(Safety)

Rxn of organometallic nucleophile with ELECTROPHILES like these:
- C=O (carbonyl)
- Epoxide
- Ester (adds TWICE)
- Carbon dioxide (followed by acid workup)
- Cyclic ester
- RX (Gilman)

(many followed by acid workup: HA. What is a good acid for this? Water will work; sometimes it will just say "acid work-up" or HA or H_3O^+ indicating a proton source.)

35

Organometallics

Carbanion C$^-$ nucleophile!

React with carbon electrophile like C=O in many functional groups (followed by acid work up with weak acid, or even just water)

Makes new carbon-carbon bond

36

Organometallics

Reagent preparation (Grignards and organolithiums and Gilman)

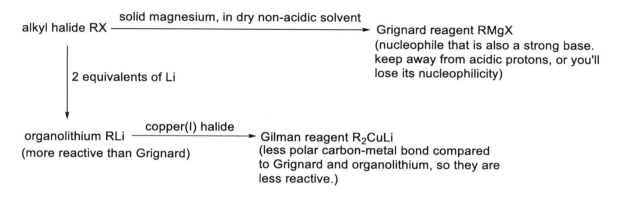

alkyl halide RX ——— solid magnesium, in dry non-acidic solvent ———→ Grignard reagent RMgX
(nucleophile that is also a strong base. keep away from acidic protons, or you'll lose its nucleophilicity)

| 2 equivalents of Li

organolithium RLi ——— copper(I) halide ———→ Gilman reagent R_2CuLi
(more reactive than Grignard) (less polar carbon-metal bond compared to Grignard and organolithium, so they are less reactive.)

37

Organometallics

Rxn ("reaction") of Grignard (or organolithium, nucleophile) with
    C=O (carbonyl: aldehyde or ketone, electrophile)

38

Organometallics

Rxn of Grignard (or RLi) with
Epoxide

39

Organometallics

Rxn of Grignard with
Ester (adds TWICE)

40

20

Organometallics

Rxn of Grignard with
Carbon dioxide (followed by acid workup)

41

Organometallics

Rxn of Grignard with
Cyclic ester

42

RXN conditions to **prepare** Organometallics

Must be dry, no acid!

Why? Organometallic reagents are VERY STRONG BASES

(Also consider if your solvent is electrophilic with a Grignard and will react with it. Always think about the structure and functional groups on your solvent.)

Examples

These reagents are prepared in (aprotic) ether solvents like diethyl ether or THF.

Organolithium example

Gilman (organocuprate) example

R₂CuLi

Made from organolithium with CuI in THF or diethylether

Less reactive than organolithium and Grignard because C-Cu bond is less polar

Useful for formation of C-C bonds with alkyl or aryl halides (not RF, not tertiary)

Gilman reagents can react **with alkyl halides.** Performed at low temperature with diethyl ether or THF as the solvent.

$$R_2CuLi \ + \ R'\text{--}X \longrightarrow R''R \ + \ RCu \ + \ LiX$$

| Gilman reagent | alkyl halide | coupling product | biproducts |

Note: Alkyl or aryl halides work

Example

45

Grignard, Organolithium and Organocuprates summary

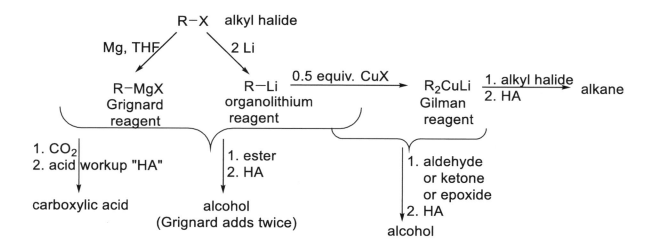

46

aura Lanni

23

Practice: what is the major isolated organic product of each reaction?

A. ~~~Br $\xrightarrow{\text{1. Mg, THF}}$ 2. HA 3. CO_2

B. ~~~Br $\xrightarrow{\text{1. Mg, THF}}$ 2. CO_2 3. H_2O

C. ~~Br $\xrightarrow{\text{1. Mg, THF}}$ 2. CO_2 3. H_2O

D. ~~~Br $\xrightarrow{\text{1. NaOMe}}$ 2. BH_3 3. H_2O_2 4. H_2CrO_4

47

Practice

$\xrightarrow[\text{Heck reaction}]{\text{PdL}_2}$

$\xrightarrow{\substack{\text{1. BH}_3 \\ \text{2. H}_2\text{O}_2, \text{NaOH}}}$

PCC

1. BrMg

2. H_2O

48

Practice

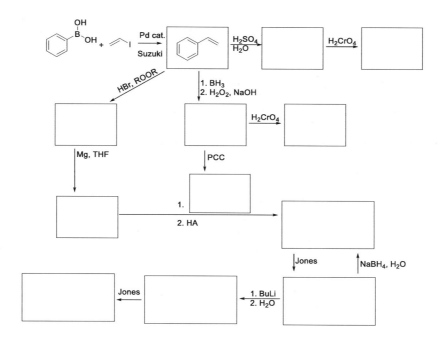

Practice

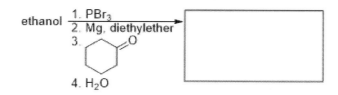

Practice

Design two ways to make 4-methyl-4-heptanol ( ) via Grignard.

Synthesis examples/reaction review

Multisteps, synthetic design, examples

Predict the major isolated organic product(s)

1-bromobutane → 1. Mg, THF
2. CO_2
3. NH_4^+(aq)
4. LAH
5. H_2O
6. H_2SO_4
7. BH_3
8. H_2O_2, ^-OH
9. PCC

?

A. (ketone structure)

B. (aldehyde structure, H–)

C. (ketone structure)

D. (aldehyde structure, H–)

E. none of these

F. more than one of these

G. (structure) Br

Self-check Practice

W 1. O_3 / 2. $(CH_3)_2S$ → X 1. CH_3Li / 2. H_3O^+

X → H_2SO_4

Z ← 1. BH_3 / 2. H_2O_2, NaOH ← Y

1. What functional group is in major product **W**?

A. Alkene
B. Secondary Alcohol
C. Primary Alcohol
D. Aldehyde
E. Epoxide

2. What functional group is in major product **X**?

A. Alkene
B. Secondary Alcohol
C. Primary Alcohol
D. Aldehyde
E. Epoxide

3. What functional group is in major product **Y**?

A. Alkene
B. Secondary Alcohol
C. Primary Alcohol
D. Aldehyde
E. Epoxide

4. What functional group is in major product **Z**?

A. Alkene
B. Secondary Alcohol
C. Primary Alcohol
D. Aldehyde
E. Epoxide

5. Which best describes the major isolated organic product (designated "Product I") of this two-step process?

(structure) C_2H_5MgBr → H_3O^+ → Product I

A. An achiral secondary alcohol
B. A chiral secondary alcohol
C. An achiral tertiary alcohol
D. A chiral tertiary alcohol
E. There is no reaction

For this series of reactions, which reagent will accomplish each step?

1-bromopropane —6.→ Product "X"

1-bromopropane —7.↓

propene —8.→ (structure) OH

19

(structure) OH —9.→ (structure) H, O

Answer choices* for reactions 6 – 9:
A. PCC
B. NaOMe
C. Mg, THF
D. 1. BH_3
   2. H_2O_2, ^-OH
E. 1. Product "X"
   2. HA

*use each answer only once

Practice

10. What functional groups will be on the major product of this reaction?

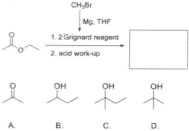

pyridinium chlorochromate (PCC)

a. Ketone and secondary alcohol
b. Ketone and tertiary alcohol
c. Aldehyde and tertiary alcohol
d. Aldehyde and ketone
e. Alcohol and alkene

11. Which most completely and correctly describes the major organic product of the reaction shown?

1. CuI (1 mole)

2 mol   Br

2.   (1 mole)

Gilman Reagent

A   B   C   D   E

12. What is the final product of this series of reaction steps?

CH_3Br

Mg, THF

1. 2 Grignard reagent

2. acid work-up

A.   B.   C.   D.

13. What is the major isolated organic product of the process shown?

1. C_2H_5MgBr

2. H_3O^+ Product

A. An achiral secondary alcohol
B. A chiral secondary alcohol
C. An achiral primary alcohol
D. A chiral primary alcohol
E. A racemic mixture

55

Moving on to new material for orgo 2...

Resonance review

Allylic halogenation

Dienes

Conjugation

Addition of HX to conjugated diene

Diels Alder

Aromaticity

UV-vis spectroscopy

56

Laura Lanni   28

Delocalized electrons and the stabilizing effect of conjugation, "resonance stabilization"

Delocalized electrons: "loose" like lone pairs or π electrons

Resonance can stabilize a charged (or neutral) particle

Conjugation: alternating sigma(σ) and pi (π) bonds

Lewis structures, resonance review, examples

Resonance review

1. may ONLY move electrons

2. cannot exceed octet

3. relative stability of resonance structures:

     a. more covalent bonds, more stable

     b. all atoms with octet, more stable

     c. charge separation decreases stability

Resonance examples and practice

Resonance practice

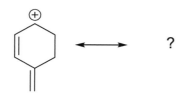

?

A

B

C

D

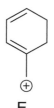

E

Allylic group

Allylic carbocation

Allylic radical

Allylic anion

Draw resonance structures

Delocalization of unpaired, lone, or pi electron(s) makes allylic particle more stable

All 3 carbon atoms are sp^2 hybridized

All 3 carbon atoms have one un-hybridized p orbital perpendicular to the plane of the atoms (π system)

61

Allylic halogenation

At room temperature alkenes react with chlorine or bromine by **addition** (orgo 1 review)

At elevated temperatures or appropriate energy (hv), **substitution at allylic position** occurs (via radical mechanism)

example and mechanism

(Note: must use low concentration of Br$_2$ or addition across double bond can occur. N-bromosuccinimide (NBS) is an alternative reagent)

62

Benzylic position is conjugated/resonance stabilized, like allylic

Dienes: hydrocarbons with 2 double bonds

Conjugated dienes:

Cumulated dienes:

Isolated dienes:

Stability from **conjugation**

Conjugated double bonds are 15 kJ/mol (3.6 kcal/mol) more stable than **isolated** double bonds.

Why?

65

s-*cis* and s-*trans* conjugated dienes

That σ bond between the two π bonds in a conjugated diene acts like a regular σ bond—it is FREE TO ROTATE.

Two conformations are possible when the 4 sp^2 carbons are coplanar: s-*cis* and s-*trans*

66

Addition of HX to conjugated dienes (can give a mixture of products)

Example / thermodynamic and kinetic control / Reaction coordinate diagram

67

Addition of HX to conjugated dienes (can give a mixture of products)

68

Diels-Alder reaction

Product: (substituted) cyclohexene

Reactants: diene and dienophile

Diene MUST be able to adopt **s-cis** conformation

General reaction/mechanism

examples

69

Diels-Alder Reactions: considerations

When an electron withdrawing group (EWG) is
attached to the dienophile, the reaction is generally
spontaneous

(red groups are electron withdrawing)

Diels-Alder reactions are **stereospecific** depending on
whether a (*E*) or (*Z*) dienophile is used

The major product of Diels-Alder can be predicted by
considering the charge distribution of the reactants
(hybrid resonance structures show partial charges on
diene dienophile carbons):

70

What is the final product in this series of 5 reactions?

Start with ethylene

1. 1,3-butadiene
2. NBS (N-bromosuccinimide) and peroxide ROOR (allylic halogenation)
3. Alkoxide base (like ⁻OMe)
4. Br$_2$, 400∘C or hv (like step 2, another allylic halogenation)
5. Repeat step 3

PRODUCT?

71

PRACTICE

A.

B.

C.

D.

1. What is the major isolated organic product when the reaction occurs hot?
2. Is the major isolated organic product the same when the reaction occurs cold?

72

Laura Lanni

36

BENZENE

Benzene is stabilized by the **delocalization** of the 6 electrons in the π system.

This inherent stability is called '**resonance stabilization**'

Because of it, the C=Cs in benzene DO NOT react like typical alkenes

73

Molecular orbitals (MOs) in benzene

Atomic orbitals   molecular orbitals

74

Aromaticity and Hückel's Rule

Hückel's Rule: among planar, monocyclic, fully conjugated polyenes, only those possessing (4n+2) π electrons, where n = whole #, will have special stability—that is, will be '*aromatic*.'

RESTATEMENT: A planar, monocyclic, continuous system of *p*-orbitals **possesses aromatic stability** when it contains (4n+2) π electrons.

Alternative statement of **aromaticity**: The molecule must contain a ring of continuously overlapping *p* orbitals AND the number of π electrons in the ring must be a Hückel number

75

Aromatic vs anti-aromatic vs non-aromatic
(most stable)   (least stable)   (no special stability/instability—in the middle)

	planar RING?	**All atoms in ring sp²?**	**(4n+2) π e⁻?**
classification			
Aromatic			
Anti-aromatic			
Non-aromatic			

76

Examples: aromatic? Antiaromatic? Nonaromatic?

	planar RING?	All atoms in ring sp²?	(4n+2) π e⁻?	Classify as...

77

MORE Examples: aromatic? Antiaromatic? Nonaromatic?

	planar RING?	All atoms in ring sp²?	(4n+2) π e⁻?	Classify as...

78

Some examples of aromatic **cations and anions**

	planar RING?	All atoms in ring sp²?	(4n+2) π e⁻?	Classify as...

79

Heterocyclic aromatics (contain N or O or S)

All of these are aromatic.
Justify each.

80

PRACTICE

HOW MANY OF THESE ARE AROMATIC?

A. 0

B. 1

C. 2

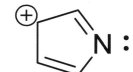

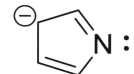

81

PRACTICE

1. In a Diels-Alder reaction where 1,3-butadiene (a molecule used in reaction in lecture this week) is the only reactant, which product may form?

none of these

A   B   C   D   E

3. Which is a valid hybrid resonance depiction of this allylic carbocation?

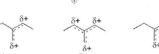

A   B   C   D

2. When 5,6-dimethyl-1,3-cyclohexadiene reacts with HBr as shown, two products may be formed. Which is a true statement about the two products?

and

Product 1   Product 2

A. They will be formed in equal amounts regardless of temperature.
B. Product 1 will be the major product at low temperatures.
C. Product 2 will be the major product at low temperatures.
D. The two products shown are identical, so there is really only one product formed.

82

PRACTICE

When 5-methyl-1,3-cyclopentadiene reacts with HBr as shown, two products may be formed. Which is a true statement about the two products?

Product 1   Product 2

A. They will be formed in equal amounts regardless of temperature.
B. Product 1 will be the major product at low temperatures.
C. Product 2 will be the major product at low temperatures.
D. The two products shown are identical, so there is really only one product formed.

In a Diels-Alder reaction where 1,3-cyclohexadiene is the only reactant, which product may form?

A   B   C   D   none of these

E

Acid and base strength—consideration of resonance, aromaticity

Ultraviolet-visible spectroscopy (UV-VIS)

See the UV Vis Addendum and video lesson posted on Blackboard.

1. Which is the weakest base (hint: most stable)?

   A.   B.   C.   D.

Practice

2. Which is not a valid resonance structure of this benzylic cation?

   A.

   B.

   C.

   D.

3. Consider the reaction of 1,4-dimethyl-1,3-cyclohexadiene with HBr. Which best describes the major organic product at each of the given temperatures?

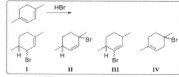

	At –40 °C	At +50 °C
A.	Product I	Product II
B.	Product III	Product II
C.	Product I	Product I
D.	Product IV	Product II
E.	Product III	Product I

4. Which statement is true regarding addition of HBr to conjugated dienes?

   A. The thermodynamic product is always the most stable alkene, whereas the kinetic product is always the 1,2-addition product
   B. The thermodynamic product is always the 1,4-addition product, whereas the kinetic product is always the 1,2-addition product
   C. The thermodynamic product is always the one with the lower transition state energy, whereas the kinetic product is always formed most quickly
   D. The thermodynamic product is always derived from the most stable carbocation, whereas the kinetic product is always derived from the least stable carbocation
   E. The thermodynamic product is always formed more slowly, whereas the kinetic product is always formed more quickly

5. What is the missing reactant needed to produce the major product indicated for this reaction? (Note: "low temp" here is −40°C.)

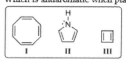

A.　　B.　　C.　　D.

none of the above

Practice

6. Which is antiaromatic when planar?

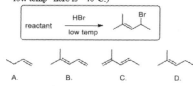

I　　II　　III

A. I only
B. II only
C. III only
D. Exactly two of them
E. None of them

7. Which of the following species adhere to the Hückel (4*n*+2) rule requirement for aromaticity?

I　　II　　III

A. Exactly two of them
B. None of them
C. I only
D. II only
E. III only

8. Which statement best describes the aromaticity and UV-vis spectra of these two substances?

I　　II

A. Both are aromatic. The longest wavelength of absorbance of I is larger than that of II.
B. Both are aromatic. The longest wavelength of absorbance of II is larger than that of I.
C. I is aromatic while II is antiaromatic. The longest wavelength of absorbance of I is larger than that of II.
D. II is aromatic while I is antiaromatic. The longest wavelength of absorbance of II is larger than that of I.
E. Both are aromatic and have no absorbance in the UV-vis region.

9. What is the missing reagent in this Diels-Alder reaction?

A. C₂H₄
B. C₂H₆
C. C₂H₂
D. cyclohexene

87

PRACTICE
Which of these has the lowest pK_a (is most acidic)? Why?

Electrophilic Aromatic Substitution (EAS)

Reactions on benzene compounds

How to functionalize benzene: EAS of benzene, mechanism

    Nitration

    Sulfonation

    Halogenation

    Friedel-Crafts alkylation

    Friedel-Crafts acylation

Alkylbenzenes by acylation/reduction (Clemmensen or Wolff-Kishner)

Subsequent EAS, directing and activating groups—making di and tri-substituted benzenes

S_NAr

89

Examples of substituted derivatives of benzene and their names
(like toluene, xylene, bromobenzene, phenol, aniline, TNT, more)

<u>R</u>   <u>name</u>

xylenes (mix of dimethylbenzenes)

90

Polyaromatics and their names
(like naphthalene, anthracene, biphenyl, more)

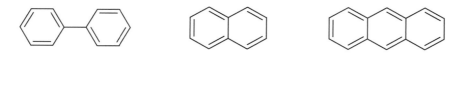

91

General mechanism of EAS   (Electrophilic Aromatic Substitution)
(Watch posted video on Blackboard)

1. A pair of electrons in the benzene π system grabs an electrophile (E⁺)
2. Deprotonation (of SAME carbon that just picked up the electrophile) restores aromaticity

92

Reaction coordinate diagram of EAS

5 EAS reactions

Nitration

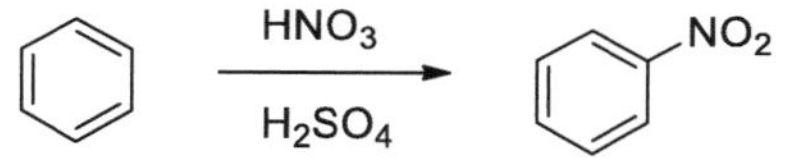

Sulfonation

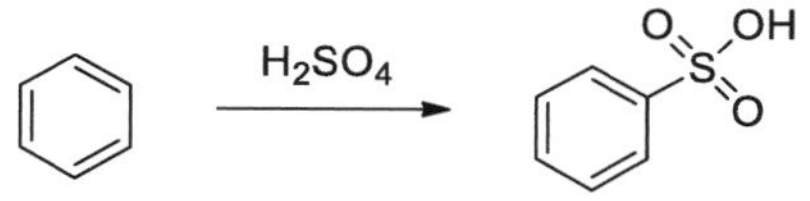

Halogenation

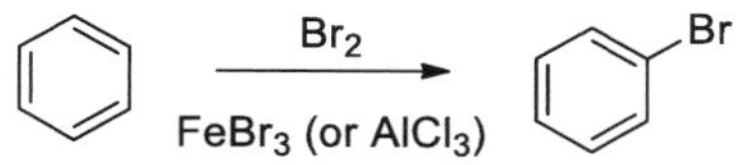

Friedel-Crafts alkylation

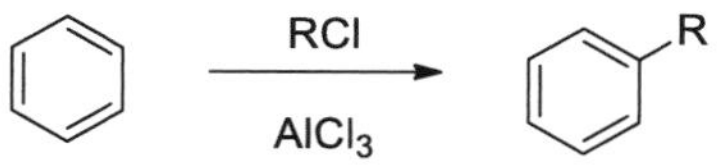

Friedel-Crafts acylation

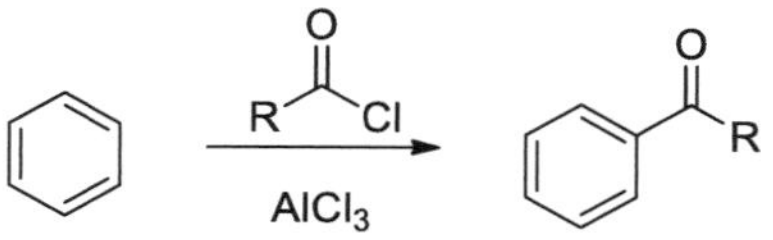

Nitration of benzene

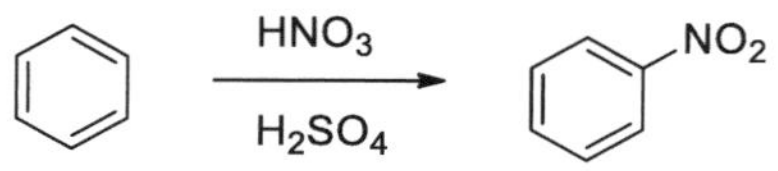

$C_6H_6 \xrightarrow[\text{H}_2\text{SO}_4]{\text{HNO}_3} C_6H_5NO_2$

Mechanism

(followed by reduction makes aniline)

Sulfonation of benzene

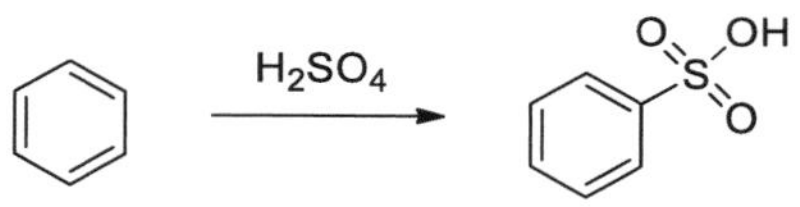

$C_6H_6 \xrightarrow{\text{H}_2\text{SO}_4} C_6H_5SO_3H$

Mechanism

Laura Lanni

Halogenation of benzene

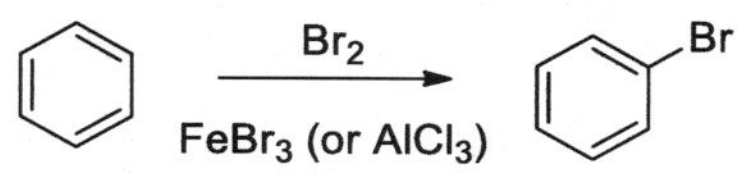

Mechanism

Friedel-Crafts alkylation

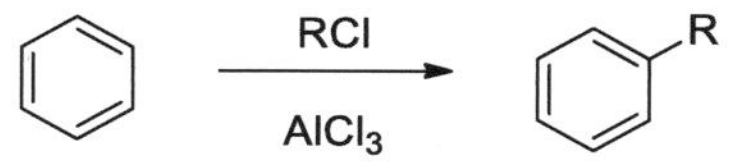

Mechanism

Friedel-Crafts alkylation

benzene $\xrightarrow[\text{AlCl}_3]{\text{RCl}}$ R-benzene

Prone to rearrangement

Example: benzene + 1-bromo-2-methylpropane, $AlCl_3$ → t-butyl benzene (Justify with mechanism)

Multiple substitutions may occur because alkyl (R) groups *activate* benzene for more additions

99

Friedel-Crafts acylation

benzene $\xrightarrow[\text{AlCl}_3]{\text{R-C(=O)-Cl}}$ benzene-C(=O)-R

NO rearrangement

Stops at one substitution

mechanism

100

Friedel-Crafts acylation

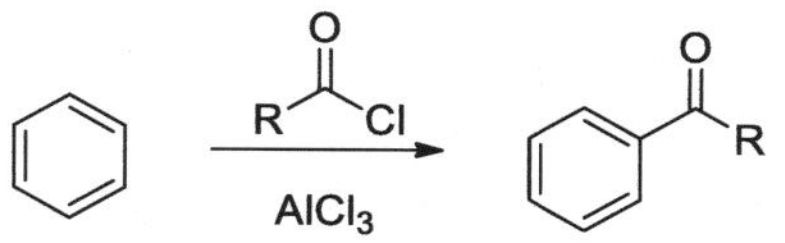

How to make acid chloride reagent from carboxylic acid—reagents and mechanism

101

Friedel-Crafts acylation

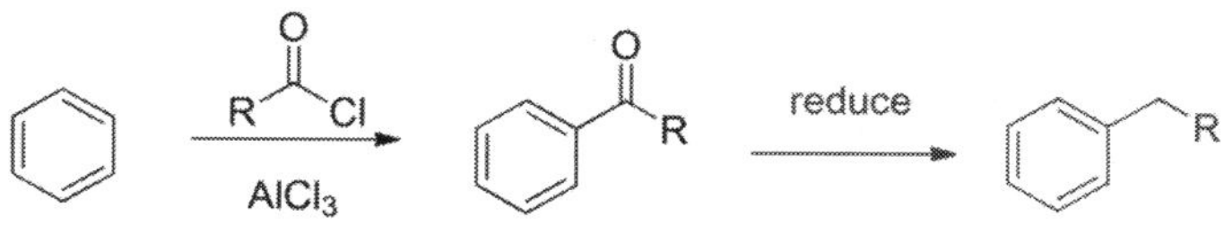

Subsequent **reduction** makes alkylated benzene

Two ways: Clemmensen or Wolff-Kishner

102

ALTERNATIVE Friedel-Crafts acylation with anhydride

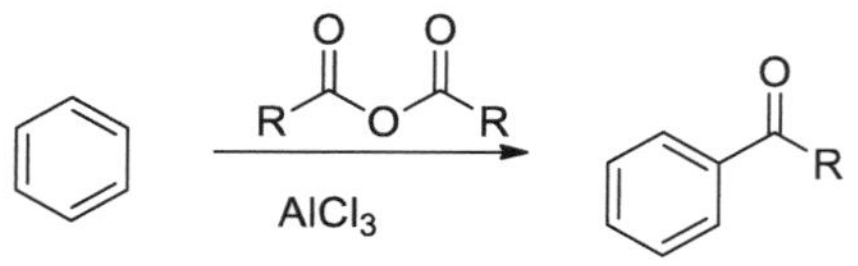

Works with succinic anhydride

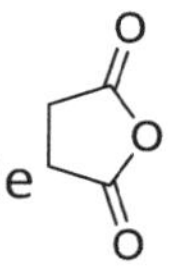

Example

Multistep

What *else* can we do?

PRACTICE

What reagents are needed for each reaction?

Reaction 1

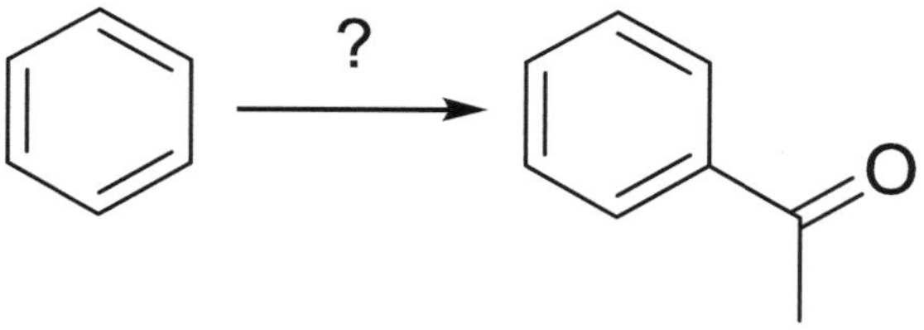

Reaction 2

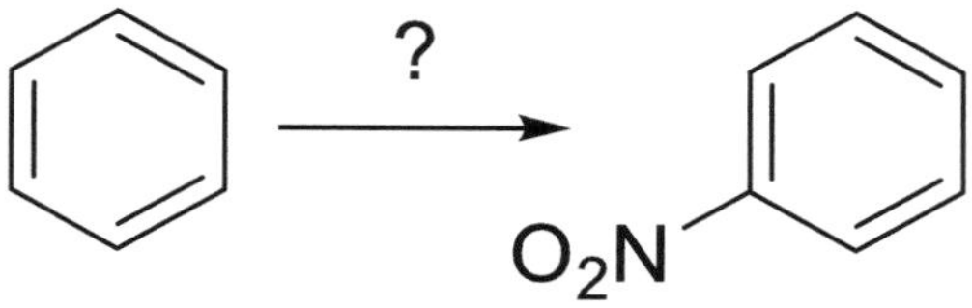

PRACTICE

Fill in the missing reagents for reactions 1-4 and the final product of the multistep synthesis in box 5

Activating and deactivating groups on benzene

Some substituents on benzene activate it toward another substitution
     (called activating groups)
     (make next EAS faster)

Some substituents on benzene deactivate it toward another substitution
     (called deactivating groups)
     (make next EAS slower)

Activating and deactivating groups on benzene

summarize activating groups—table in text

Most activating groups are *ortho, para* **directors**

Most deactivating groups are *meta* **directors**

ortho   A   ortho

meta   meta

para

107

Activating and deactivating groups on benzene

	group	how does it direct next EAS?
Most activating		
Moderately activating		
Activating		
(all compared to H)		
Deactivating		
Moderately deactivating		
Most deactivating		

108

Activating and deactivating groups on benzene
Examples

Activating and deactivating groups on benzene
Examples

Activating and deactivating groups on benzene

Design a series of synthetic steps starting from benzene to make this target molecule

PRACTICE

Fill in reagents for reactions 1-4

Reaction 1 → Reaction 2 →

Reaction 3 → Reaction 4 →

Laura Lanni

5

Activating and deactivating groups on benzene

Why are some groups activating and others deactivating?

Need to look at **transition states**.

Activating groups donate electron density to the ring via induction and/or resonance, stabilizing the transition state in the slow first step, thereby reducing the activation energy and making the slow step occur faster.

(Deactivating groups have the opposite effect: electron withdrawing, destabilize TS, next EAS slower.)

113

Activating and deactivating groups on benzene

How does first group on benzene direct addition of subsequent groups?

Look at NUMBER (and stability) of resonance structures of carbocation intermediate

Meta directors (see subsequent slide)

ortho/para directors (see subsequent slide)

114

Meta directors (EWG, deactivators)

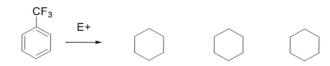

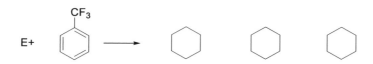

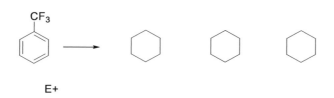

ortho, para-directors (EDG, almost all activators)

Adding 3rd group on benzene

What if the first two groups direct to DIFFERENT positions?

The stronger activator will win (top of the list)

Note: substitution between two meta groups is highly unlikely.

117

PRACTICE

Design a series of synthetic steps to make each of these target molecules from benzene

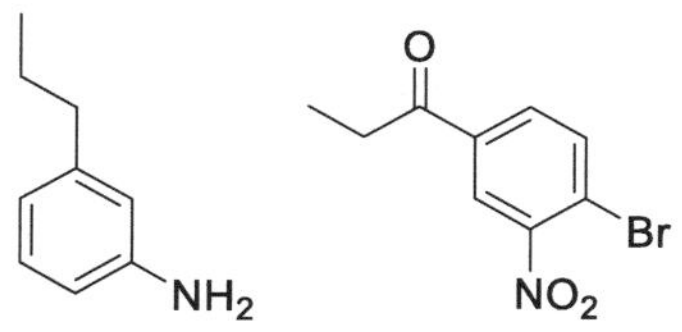

118

Birch reduction

Benzene $\xrightarrow{\text{Na, NH}_3\text{, ROH}}$ 1,4-cyclohexadiene

mechanism

Oxidation of alkyl benzenes (aka benzylic oxidation)

Alkyl benzene → benzoic acid

Benzyl alcohol → benzaldehyde

Free radical halogenation of alkyl benzenes (aka benzylic bromination)

Use Br_2, hv, or NBS on alkyl benzene to brominate benzylic position

121

Polymerization of styrene (review from orgo 1)

122

$S_N Ar$ Nucleophilic aromatic substitution

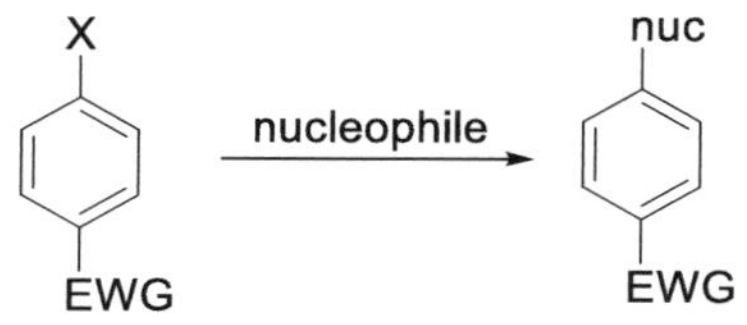

(x is leaving group and must be *ortho* or *para* to EWG)

Example and mechanism

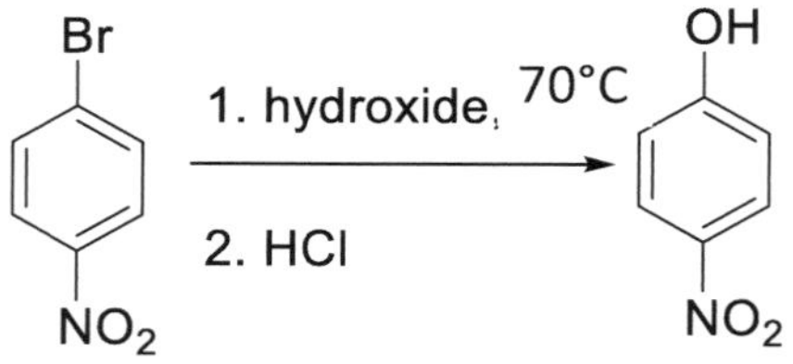

1. hydroxide, 70°C

2. HCl

123

$S_N Ar$ examples

124

PRACTICE

Which product(s) can be formed?

Why is it formed?

toluene $\xrightarrow{\text{AlCl}_3}$

A.

B.

C.

125

Review/practice

Which statement is true regarding addition of HBr to conjugated dienes?

A. The thermodynamic product is always the most stable alkene, whereas the kinetic product is always the 1,2-addition product
B. The thermodynamic product is always the 1,4-addition product, whereas the kinetic product is always the 1,2-addition product
C. The thermodynamic product is always the one with the lower transition state energy, whereas the kinetic product is always formed most quickly
D. The thermodynamic product is always derived from the most stable carbocation, whereas the kinetic product is always derived from the least stable carbocation
E. The thermodynamic product is always formed more slowly, whereas the kinetic product is always formed more quickly

Hint: consider 2,3,5-trimethyl-2,4-hexadiene + HCl

126

3 more EAS synthesis examples (Retrosynthesis)

1. 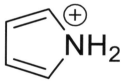 COOH / Cl benzene ring ⟹ toluene (methylbenzene)

2. 2-bromo-4-nitrotoluene ⟹ toluene

3. 4-chloro-2-nitrobenzoic acid ⟹ toluene

Practice/review

Is this aromatic, antiaromatic, or non-aromatic?

Practice: Design a synthesis to convert 2-bromopropane to propanal?

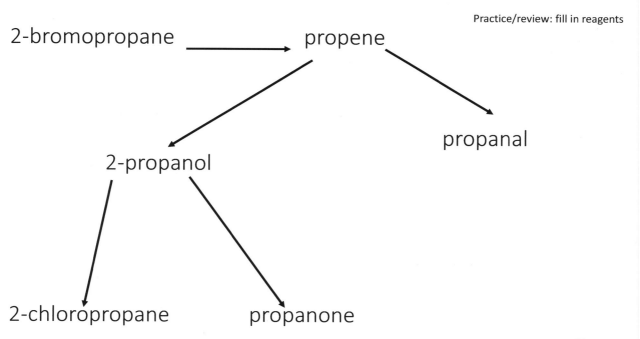

129

Practice/review: fill in reagents

2-bromopropane ⟶ propene

propene ⟶ 2-propanol

propene ⟶ propanal

2-propanol ⟶ 2-chloropropane

2-propanol ⟶ propanone

130

Practice:
Starting with benzene, what will each of these series of synthetic steps produce?

1. 1. AlCl₃, [acyl chloride]
    2. Br₂, FeBr₃
    3. Zn(Hg), HCl

2. 1. AlCl₃, [acyl chloride]
    2. MeMgBr
    3. acid work up
    4. H₂SO₄

3. 1. HNO₃, H₂SO₄
    2. Ni, H₂
    3. NH₄Cl(aq) (weak acid)
    4. Br₂, FeBr₃
    5. weak base

4. 1. MeCl, AlCl₃
    2. AlCl₃, [acyl chloride]
    3. NaBH₄, H₂O
    4. H₂SO₄

131

PRACTICE

1. At least 7 ways to make 2-methyl-2-pentanol

2. From ethene, make

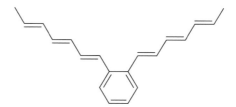

132

6

PRACTICE

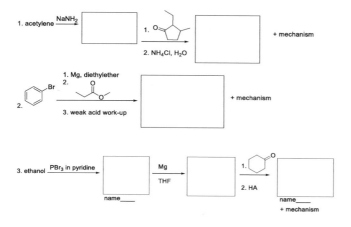

1. acetylene $\xrightarrow{\text{NaNH}_2}$ [ ] $\xrightarrow[\text{2. NH}_4\text{Cl, H}_2\text{O}]{\text{1.}}$ [ ] + mechanism

2. [ ]—Br $\xrightarrow[\text{3. weak acid work-up}]{\substack{\text{1. Mg, diethylether} \\ \text{2.}}}$ [ ] + mechanism

3. ethanol $\xrightarrow{\text{PBr}_3 \text{ in pyridine}}$ [ ] name___ $\xrightarrow[\text{THF}]{\text{Mg}}$ [ ] $\xrightarrow[\text{2. HA}]{\text{1.}}$ [ ] name___ + mechanism

4. Design a series of synthetic steps to make 4-methyl-4-heptanol via Grignard reaction

a. with ester
b. with ketone
c. with different ketone

5. 1-bromobutane $\rightarrow$
1. Mg, THF
2. carbon dioxide
3. acid work-up
4. LAH
5. dilute sulfuric acid
6. PCC
[ ]

6. 1-bromobutane $\rightarrow$
1. Mg, THF
2. carbon dioxide
3. acid work-up
4. LAH
5. concentrated sulfuric acid
6. Br$_2$
7. 3 NaNH$_2$
8. HA
9. NaH
10. product from number 5
11. HA
[ ]

133

Practice

1-3 Choose the best reagents for each numbered step that will give the best yield for the following synthesis.
Each number corresponds to the question number.

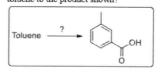

1 → 2 → 3 →

A. HNO$_3$, H$_2$SO$_4$
B. CH$_3$COCl, AlCl$_3$
C. NH$_2$NH$_2$, KOH, heat
D. Na, NH$_3$, MeOH
E. Br$_2$, FeBr$_3$

4,5 Give the correct reagent for each numbered reaction. The number corresponds to the question number.

A. HBr
B. HBr, ROOR
C. Br$_2$ (dark)
D. Br$_2$, hv
E. Br$_2$, FeBr$_3$

6. Which reaction sequence is necessary to convert toluene to the product shown?

Toluene $\xrightarrow{?}$ [ ]

A. 1. KMnO$_4$ 2. CH$_3$C(O)Cl, AlCl$_3$
B. 1. CH$_3$Cl, AlCl$_3$ 2. KMnO$_4$
C. 1. CH$_3$C(O)Cl, AlCl$_3$ 2. MnO$_2$
D. 1. CH$_3$Cl, AlCl$_3$ 2. MnO$_2$
E. 1. KMnO$_4$ 2. CH$_3$Cl, AlCl$_3$

7. What is the final product for the given sequence of reactions?

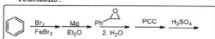

$\xrightarrow[\text{FeBr}_3]{\text{Br}_2}$ $\xrightarrow[\text{Et}_2\text{O}]{\text{Mg}}$ $\xrightarrow[\text{2. H}_2\text{O}]{\text{Ph}}$ $\xrightarrow{\text{PCC}}$ $\xrightarrow{\text{H}_2\text{SO}_4}$

8. Which is a major product of this Friedel-Crafts alkylation?

bromobenzene $\xrightarrow[\text{AlCl}_3]{\text{1-chloro-2-methylpentane}}$?

134

9. When benzene is reacted with HNO₃ and H₂SO₄, which electrophile is generated and reacts with benzene as part of the mechanism that leads to the major product?

A. Proton, H⁺
B. Sulfonium, [HSO₃]⁺
C. Sulfonic, [SO₂]⁺
D. Nitrosulfonic, [H₂SONO₂]⁺
E. Nitronium, [NO₂]⁺

10. When benzene reacts with HNO₃ and H₂SO₄, what is produced?

A. anisole
B. phenol
C. benzene sulfonic acid
D. nitrobenzene
E. aniline

11. When nitrobenzene reacts with H₂ and nickel what is produced?

A. anisole
B. phenol
C. benzene sulfonic acid
D. xylene
E. aniline

12. Which of the following is the IUPAC name of a compound that can be prepared as the major product of Friedel-Crafts alkylation upon a single EAS reaction of benzene with AlCl₃ and an alkyl chloride?

A. Ethyl benzene
B. Propylbenzene
C. Butylbenzene
D. Pentylbenzene
E. All of these can be made as the major product

13. Which compound is the reactant for this reaction?

14. At which carbon will a hydrogen be substituted with an electrophile most rapidly *via* an electrophilic aromatic substitution mechanism?

Aldehydes and Ketones: Nucleophilic addition to carbonyl

Introduction to aldehydes and ketones, structures, nomenclature

Synthesis of aldehydes and ketones

Nucleophilic addition to aldehydes and ketones

Addition of alcohol to C=O → hemiacetal and acetal formation (mech)

Addition of amine to C=O → imine or enamine (mech) (reductive amination)

Addition of HCN to C=O → cyanohydrin (mech?)

Addition of ylides to C=O (Wittig and Horner-Emmons-Wadsworth)

Oxidation of aldehydes (review)

Some review: Grignard (and other organometallics), reductions

Aldehydes and ketones: examples and nomenclature

Aldehydes

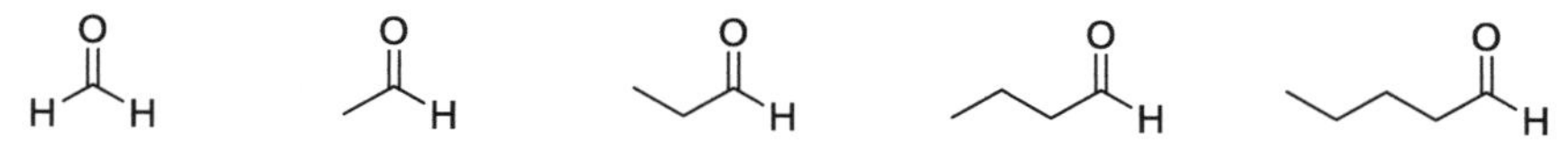

Ketones

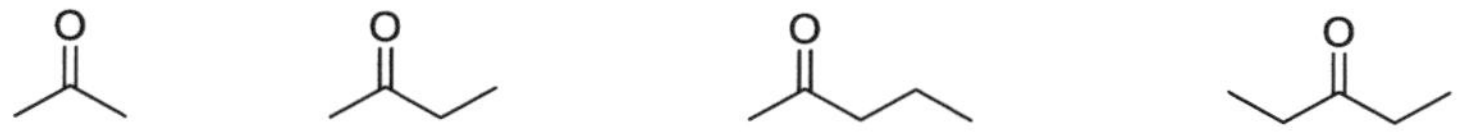

examples

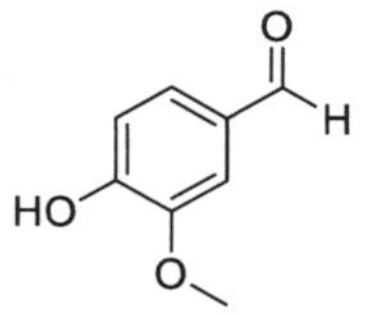

vanillin 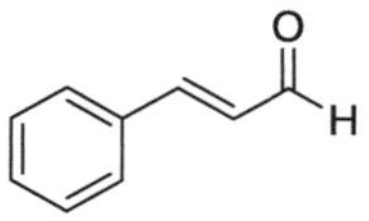   cinnamaldehyde

137

Nucleophilic addition to carbonyl (review)

Mechanism

About the nucleophile:

138

Nucleophilic addition to carbonyl--mechanisms

Strong anion nucleophile (like $^-$OH, $^-$OR alkoxide, $^-$H hydride (LAH), $^-$C (Grignard))

Weak (neutral) nucleophile (like water, alcohol, ammonia, amine)

139

Nucleophilic addition to carbonyl—3 considerations

Often reversible

Aldehydes are more reactive than ketones (why?)

Oxygen and nitrogen nucleophiles can ADD TWICE

140

Example of oxygen nucleophile adding twice to C=O

Formation of hemiacetal and acetal by

$2 \text{ ROH} + \underset{\substack{\text{aldehyde} \\ \text{or ketone}}}{\underset{\text{R'} \quad \text{R''}}{\overset{\text{O}}{\parallel}}} \quad \underset{\longleftarrow}{\overset{\text{HA}}{\longrightarrow}} \quad \underset{\substack{\text{hemiacetal} \\ \text{(from 1st addition)}}}{\underset{\text{R'} \quad \text{R''}}{\overset{\text{HO} \quad \text{OR}}{\diagup}}} \quad \longrightarrow \quad \underset{\substack{\text{acetal} \\ \text{(after 2nd addition)}}}{\underset{\text{R'} \quad \text{R''}}{\overset{\text{RO} \quad \text{OR}}{\diagup}}}$

alcohol

Acid-catalyzed acetal formation: example and mechanism

$$\underset{H}{\overset{O}{\parallel}} \xrightarrow[\text{HA (catalyst)}]{\text{ROH (2 eq)}} \underset{H}{\overset{\text{RO} \quad \text{OR}}{\diagup}}$$

141

Acetal from carbonyl and 2 equiv. alcohol: mechanism

Proton transfer

Nuc attack

Proton transfers

Water leaves

Nuc attack

Proton transfer

142

Acid-catalyzed acetal formation—notes and details

Very important mechanism
Useful reaction for protection/deprotection of C=O

Intramolecular acid-catalyzed reaction→ hemiacetal (later)

Equilibrium control—LeChatelier's principle

To convert acetal back to C=O, just add water, or dilute acid

Acetal as protecting group--Cyclic acetal formation using small diol (example) (mechanism if desired)

acetal—three examples (YOU practice the mechanisms)

What is produced in each reaction?

1.

H_2SO_4

2.

acetone and sulfuric acid

3.

methanol

Sulfuric acid

Acetal as protecting group

methyl 2-oxocyclohexanecarboxylate

1. LAH
2. HA
$\longrightarrow$?

1. 1,3-propanediol, HA
2. LAH
3. HA
$\longrightarrow$?

145

Synthesis of aldehydes and ketones (review and new)

Hydration of alkyne (orgo 1)
Markovnikov and anti-Markovnikov...both involve tautomerization

Oxidation of alcohol (orgo 1)

Oxidation (ozonolysis) of alkene (orgo 1)

Friedel-Crafts Acylation (orgo 2)

Reduction of esters, acid chlorides, nitriles with DIBAL-H (or $LiAlH(OtBu)_3$)
DIBAL-H = diisobutylaluminum hydride

146

Example of nitrogen nucleophile adding twice to C=O

Imine formation (aka Shiff base)

$$R-C(=O)-R_1 \xrightarrow[\text{HA (trace)}]{H_2N-R_2} R-C(=N-R_2)-R_1$$

For mechanism, look for clues

*oxygen is gone in product (likely protonated, left as water)

*nitrogen lost both of its Hs—deprotonation steps

(So mechanism involves nucleophilic attack on C=O and multiple protonation and deprotonation steps)

example and mechanism

Note: imines are unstable and can be easily converted back to carbonyl and primary amine by acid-catalyzed hydrolysis.

147

Example of nitrogen nucleophile adding twice to C=O: MECHANISM

Imine formation (aka Shiff base)

$$R-C(=O)-R_1 \xrightarrow[\substack{\text{HA} \\ \text{(trace)}}]{H_2N-R_2} R-C(=N-R_2)-R_1$$

example and mechanism

148

Example of nitrogen nucleophile adding twice to C=O

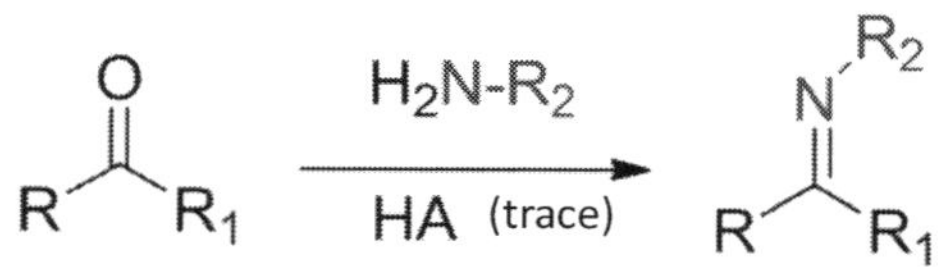

R-C(=O)-R$_1$ + H$_2$N-R$_2$ → (HA trace) → R-C(=N-R$_2$)-R$_1$

Note: imines are unstable and can be easily converted back to carbonyl and primary amine by acid-catalyzed hydrolysis.

149

PRACTICE

What is the major isolated organic product? (and write out the mechanism)

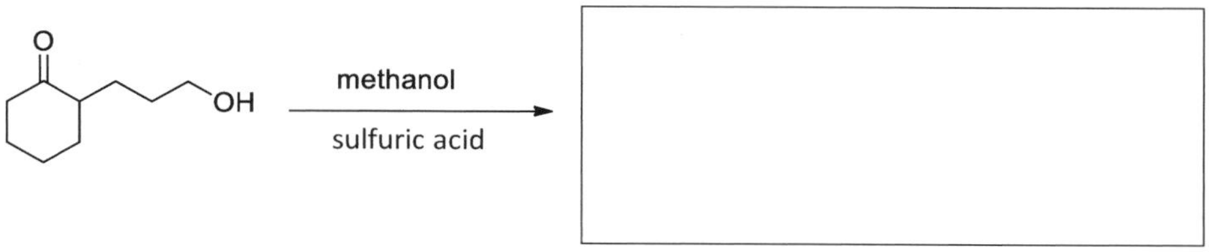

cyclohexanone with propanol chain (OH) → methanol / sulfuric acid → [ ]

150

practice

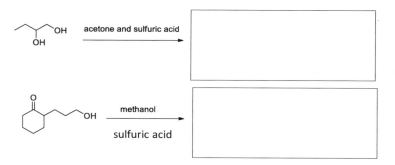

acetone and sulfuric acid

methanol

sulfuric acid

After imine formation: reductive amination

Very useful reaction for making desired **amine** from C=O

Converts imine (or enamine) to amine using sodium borohydride, or H_2 with Pd or Pt, or other reducers like $NaBH_3CN$

examples

NH_3 → $NaBH_3CN, [H^+]$ →

CH_3NH_2 → $NaBH_3CN, [H^+]$ →

$(CH_3)_2NH$ → $NaBH_3CN, [H^+]$ →

Laura Lanni

Enamine formation

Imines are formed when carbonyl reacts with **primary** amine nucleophile.

With **secondary** amine nucleophile, enamine is formed.

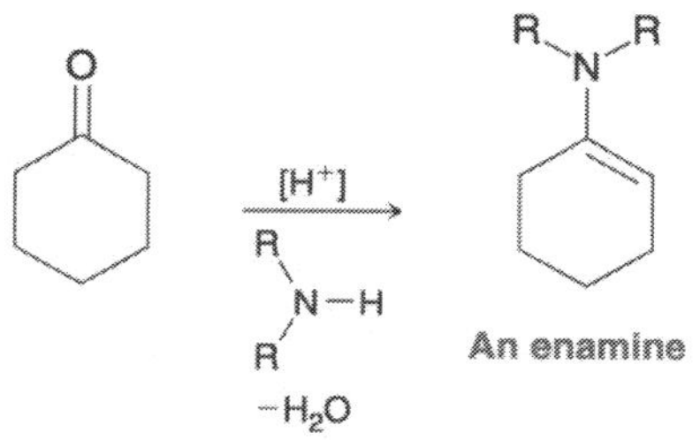

An enamine

153

Nitrogen Nucleophiles

aldehyde/ketone reacts with a **2° amine** to form an **enamine**:

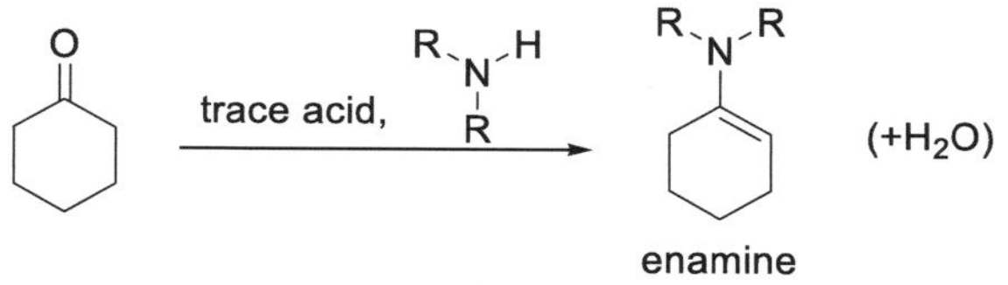

enamine

The reaction requires acidic conditions to work; the mechanism is identical to imine formation, except for the last step.

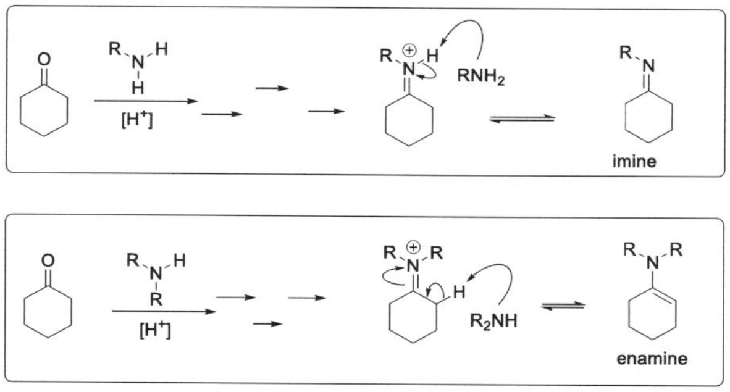

imine

enamine

154

Nitrogen Nucleophiles: Wolff-Kishner (review / add mechanism)

Wolff-Kishner reduction is a two-step synthesis, converting a **ketone to an alkane**:

First step is imine formation between the ketone and hydrazine (which is like a primary amine)

Second reaction involves proton transfers and an elimination

155

hydrolysis of acetals, imines, enamines (conversion back to carbonyl)

Acetal (or ketal) back to aldehyde (or ketone)—just add water, low pH. (Won't hydrolyze under basic conditions)

Imine or enamine back to aldehyde or ketone (and amine)—like acetal, add dilute aqueous acid. "H_2O, HA" or "[H+]"

Mechanism: proton transfer number 1, lose LG, nuc attack, proton transfer x2, lose LG, proton transfer number 4

156

Wittig reaction: makes C=C bond

Carbonyl (aldehyde or ketone) converted to alkene

Can be used to preferentially form Z-alkene

RCH_2X → 1. PPh_3 2. BuLi 3. (carbonyl R_1, R_2)

product: C with R, R_1, R_2

Reagents: 1. (alkyl halide + triphenylphosphine), 2. butyl lithium (base), 3. carbonyl

Stepwise. Order is very important.

Examples and mechanism

157

examples

PPh₃
1. 1-bromopropane
2. butyl lithium
3. cyclohexanone

[ ]

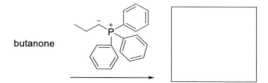 butanone

[ ]

(cyclopentane)—Br
1. PPh₃
2. butyl lithium

[ ]   butanal   [ ]

158

Modification to Wittig reaction: HWE

If the E alkene is desired, it can often be formed by using the **H**orner-**E**mmons-**W**adsworth modification to the Wittig reaction may work

Uses $P(OEt)_3$ instead of PPh_3

1. $R\diagdown X$
2. BuLi

$R\diagdown P(OEt)_2$

$^1R\diagdown\!\!\!\!\overset{O}{\diagdown}R^2$

(major product E-alkene when applicable)

Examples (no mech required)

159

Synthesis of alkenes via Wittig vs. Horner-Emmons-Wadsworth

1. $P(OEt)_3$

2. butyl lithium

3. butanone

Compare to Wittig

1. PPh_3

2. butyl lithium

3. butanone

160

Oxidation of aldehyde to carboxylic acid

Convert aldehyde to carboxylic acid

Exposure to air (slow)

Use KMnO$_4$, KOH   or   Ag$_2$O, KOH   (fast)

161

recap of reactions with aldehyde or ketone (so far)

Make aldehydes or ketones (5 or 6 ways)

Make geminal diol

Make acetal, ketal, hemiacetal, hemiketal (cyclic or not)

Make imine, enamine

Reductive amination

Wolff-Kishner

Hydrolysis of acetal, imine

Wittig and HWE

Reduction of ketones and aldehydes to alcohols

Grignard and organometallic nucleophiles, then acid workup

Oxidize aldehyde

162

Multistep syntheses/Retrosynthesis examples

3-methylcyclohexene

1. OsO₄

2. benzaldehyde, HA

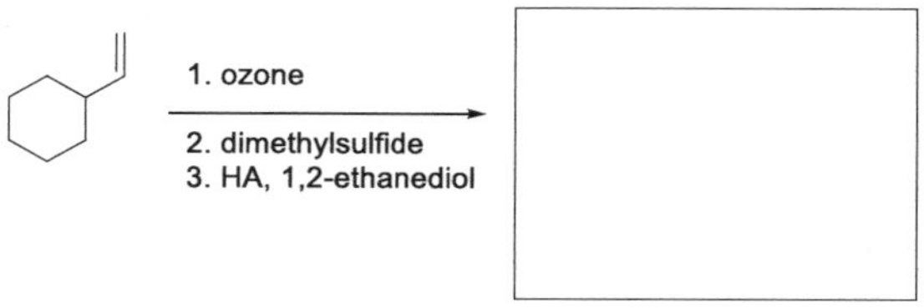

1. ozone

2. dimethylsulfide
3. HA, 1,2-ethanediol

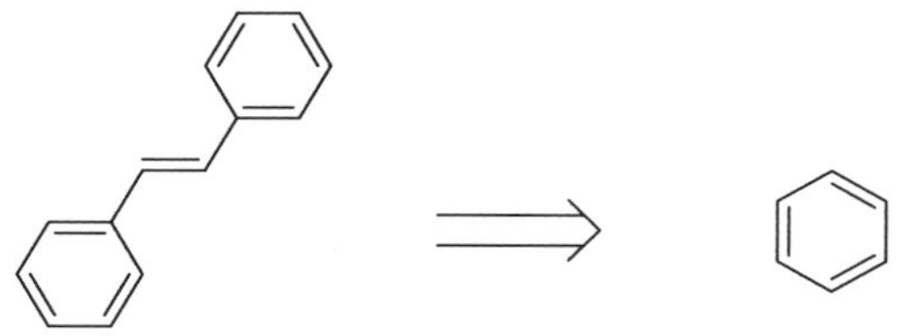

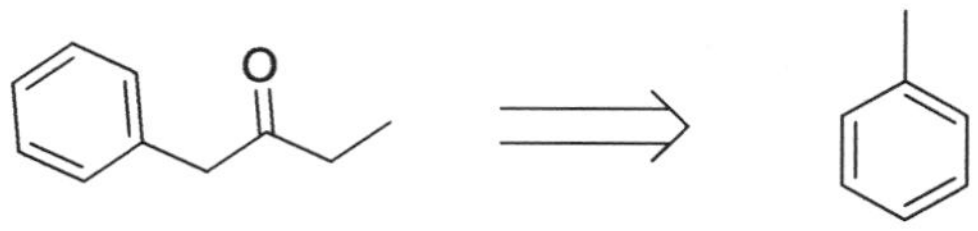

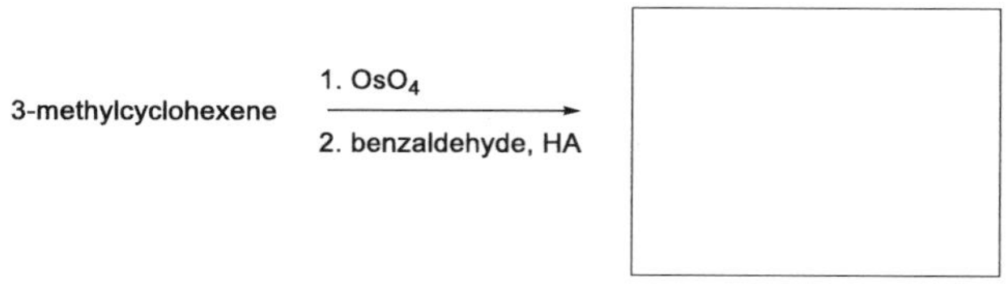

163

Multistep syntheses/Retrosynthesis examples

Start with benzene and design synthetic steps to make each

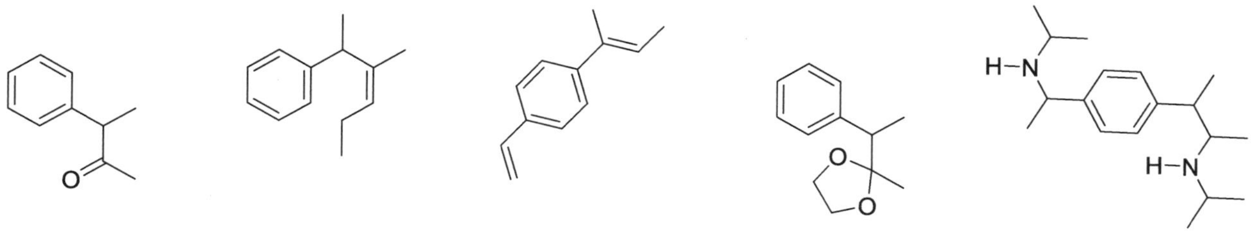

164

PRACTICE

Write the mechanism for these reactions.

Indicate flow of electrons clearly with arrows. Indicate all formal charges.

1. Propanal with acid catalyst and 2 equivalents ethanol to make the appropriate acetal.

2. Propanal with trace acid catalyst with ethylamine ($CH_3CH_2NH_2$) to make the appropriate imine.

165

1. To convert butanone to either imine or enamine, trace acid with _____ are added. Which elementary step is *different* between the two mechanisms?

	Imine	Enamine	Mechanism
A.	1° amine	2° amine	last step
B.	2° amine	1° amine	last step
C.	1° amine	3° amine	last step
D.	2° amine	3° amine	none/all same
E.	1° amine	2° amine	none/all same

2. Which statement is(are) true?
   I. 2-pentanol can be converted to pentanal with PCC (pyridinium chlorochromate).
   II. 1-pentanol can be converted to pentanal with H_2CrO_4 (chromic acid).
   III. 2-pentanone can be converted to 2-pentanol with sodium borohydride.

   A. I
   B. II
   C. III
   D. Exactly two are true.
   E. All three are true.

Practice

3. Which series of reaction steps will complete this multistep synthesis?

Part I

"Product W"

Part II   Target product

	A.	B.	C.	D.	E.
Part I:	Jones	Jones	NaBH$_4$, MeOH	Jones	Jones
Part II: start with	ethene and add:	propene	ethene	ethene	ethene
	1. HBr	1. HBr	1. Br$_2$, dark	1. Br$_2$, hv	1. HBr
	2. PPh$_3$	2. PPh$_3$	2. PPh$_3$	2. PPh$_3$	2. PPh$_3$
	3. BuLi	3. BuLi	3. BuLi	3. BuLi	3. BuOH
	4. "W"	4. "W"	4. "W"	4. "W"	4. "W"

166

Amines

The nitrogen of an amine is a trigonal pyramidal nucleophile with a lone pair of electrons.

Amines are amphoteric. With acid, amines are basic. With base, amines are acidic.

Amines

naming amines

pKa, acidity and basicity

Carboxylic acids and derivatives

Nomenclature
Preparation
Acyl substitution—nucleophilic addition/elimination at acyl C

RCOOH derivatives: [how to make, interconvert, hydrolyze back to RCOOH]
      Acyl chlorides (acid chlorides)
      Acid anhydrides
      Esters
      Amides

Decarboxylation of β-ketoacids: _ _ _ _ _ _ _ _ _ _ _

169

RCOOH derivatives
Nucleophilic addition-elimination at acyl carbon

carboxylic acid: parent to other functional groups called 'carboxylic acid derivatives'

acyl carbon

170

5 RCOOH derivatives

Acid (acyl) chloride

Anhydride

Ester

Nitrile

amide

Nomenclature/examples

Esters

Anhydrides

amides

Laura Lanni

Back to RCOOH

Acidity, pK_a
Substitution influence on pK_a

Dicarboxylic acids: OMSGA and one more (terephthalic acid)
Oxalic
Malonic
Succinic
Glutaric
Adipic acids

173

Preparation of RCOOH—review

Oxidation of alkenes (or alkynes)
Oxidation of 1° alcohols
Oxidation of aldehydes
Oxidation at benzylic position
Hydrolysis of nitrile
Grignard with carbon dioxide and acid W.U.

174

PRACTICE: What is the major organic isolated product?

butanone $\dfrac{\text{1. NaBH}_4\text{, MeOH}}{\begin{array}{l}\text{2. HBr}\\\text{3. PPh}_3\\\text{4. BuLi}\\\text{5. 3-methylbutanone}\end{array}}$?

A.   (Z)-3,4,5-triimethyl-2-hexene
B.   (Z)-3,4-dimethylhexene
C.   (Z)-2,3,4-triimethylhexane
D.   (Z)-2,3,4-triimethyl-3-hexane
E.   (E)-3,4-dimethylhexene
F.   (E)-2,3,4-triimethylhexane
G.   (E)-3,4,5-triimethylhexene
H.   (E)-2,3,4-trimethylhexene
I.   (E)-2,3,4-trimethyl-3-hexene
J.   (Z)-2,3,4-trimethylhexene
K.   (Z)-2,3,4-trimethyl-2-hexene
L.   (Z)-2,3,4-trimethyl-3-hexene
M.   (Z)-3,4,5-triimethylhexene
N.   None of these

Acyl substitution—addition-elimination at the acyl C

General mechanism

****Synthesis of acyl derivatives requires that the reactant has a better leaving group than the product****

Acyl substitution—examples

Acid chloride to carboxylic acid (mech)

Carboxylic acid to acid chloride (review)

177

Relative reactivity of acid derivatives

| acid chloride | anhydride | ester | amide (and nitriles) |

most reactive ◄————————————————————— least reactive

Leaving group: Cl⁻   carboxylate   alkoxide   amide

Synthesis of derivatives-- less reactive derivatives can be made from more reactive ones, but the reverse is generally not true (in a single step).

Example: can make ester from acid chloride.

178

Acid chlorides

Synthesis

Use

hydrolysis

Acid chlorides

Synthesis RCOOH to RCOCl with PCl_3 (instead of thionyl chloride)

Anhydrides

Synthesis

Use

hydrolysis

181

esters

Synthesis (2 ways)

Acid chloride and alcohol

Carboxylic acid and alcohol: Fischer esterification

182

esters

Cyclic esterification—makes lactone

esters

Hydrolysis (needs acid or basic catalyst) (aka "saponification")

amides

Synthesis (2 ways)

Acid chloride and excess amine

RCOOH + amine, with DCC (next slide)

185

DCC promoted amide synthesis from RCOOH

Complete the mechanism by adding arrows and formal charges to these elementary steps

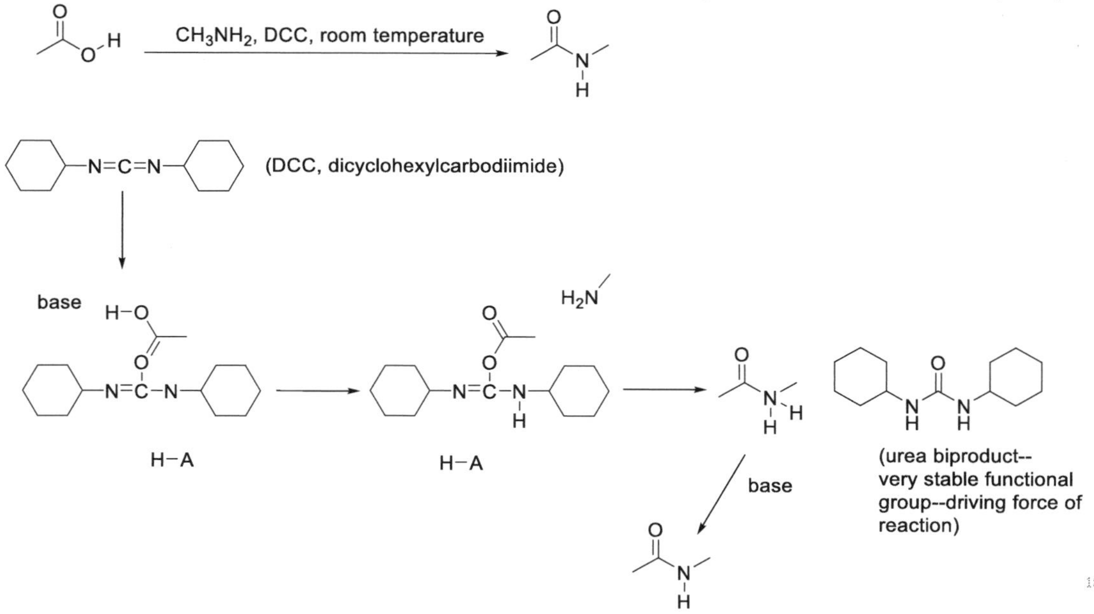

CH₃NH₂, DCC, room temperature

(DCC, dicyclohexylcarbodiimide)

base   H–O

H–A   H–A

base

(urea biproduct--
very stable functional
group--driving force of
reaction)

186

amides

Hydrolysis (acid cat and HEAT, mech)

187

PRACTICE

What is the final product (and can you draw the products after each reaction)?

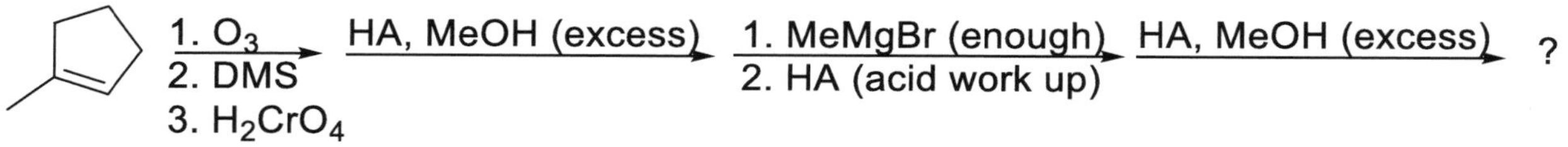

188

Multistep practice

Make from benzene and succinic anhydride

Make (structure: butanoyl anilide, CH₃CH₂CH₂C(=O)NH–C₆H₅) from acetylene and benzene

What is the final product?

(cyclopentene with methyl substituent)

1. O₃
2. DMS
3. H₂CrO₄

→ HA, MeOH (excess)

1. MeMgBr (enough)
2. HA (acid work up)

→ HA, MeOH (excess) → ?

Trans-esterification: conversion of one ester to another ester using acid catalyst and alcohol

HA (or base catalyst), ROH → (+ethanol)

Example: transesterification of triglycerides produces biodeisel

[H+]
excess
MeOH

mixture of methyl esters of fatty acids: biodeisel

191

A map
of functional group interconversions

(Not all rxns are listed. You can fill in any blanks with your lecture notes.
Practice writing the mechanisms until the obvious pattern of the general mechanism is clear...addition/elimination with logical protonations and deprotonations.)

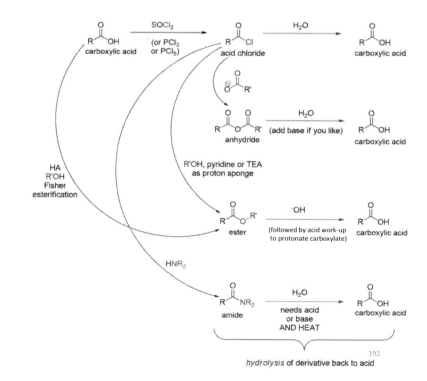

192

hydrolysis of derivative back to acid

Retrosynthesis/multistep example to make an amide

193

Decarboxylation of β-ketoacid ($-CO_2$)

Use heat

Mechanism

Review tautomerization

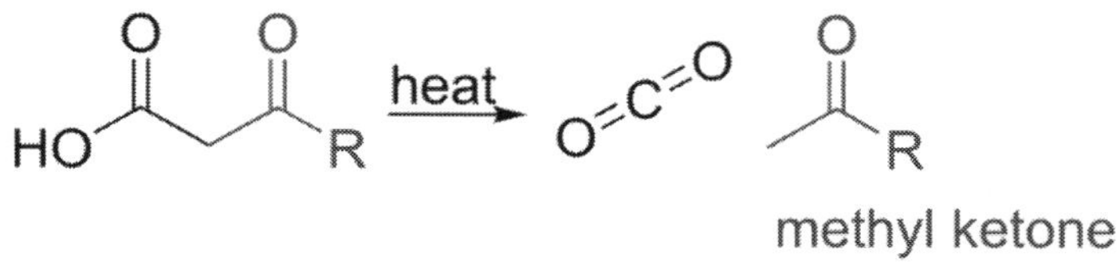

methyl ketone

194

Polyesters and polyamides

Difunctional monomers (some examples shown here) can combine to make step-growth polymers (aka condensation polymers)

Will make **polyester**

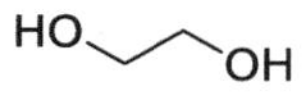

HO⌒OH

1,2-ethanediol

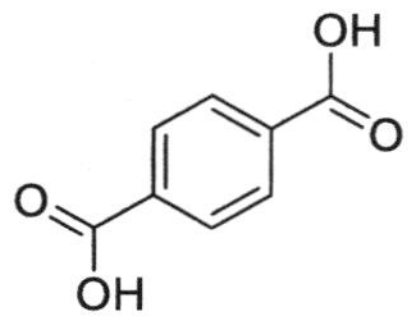

terepthalic acid

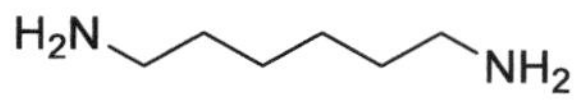

H₂N~~~NH₂

1,6-hexanediamine

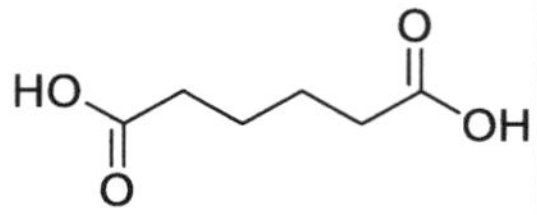

adipic acid

Will make polyamide (polypeptide)

Polyester example: PET

Monomers

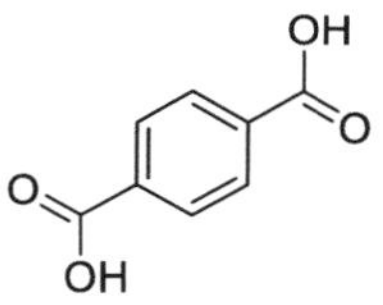

terepthalic acid

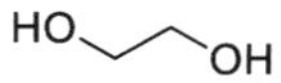

HO⌒OH

1,2-ethanediol

polymer repeating unit

Polyamide example: Nylon 6,6

Monomers

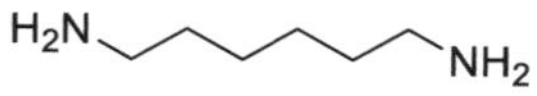

1,6-hexanediamine

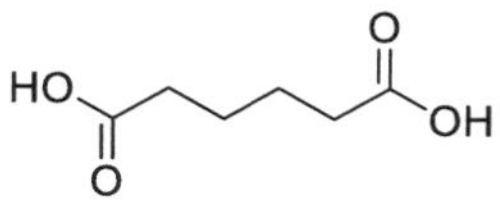

adipic acid

polymer repeating unit

Check understanding of condensation polymerization by doing an example BACKWARDS

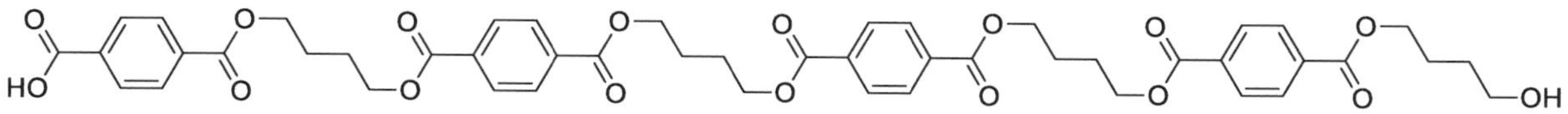

Place large square brackets to indicate the repeating unit

Draw and name the two monomers

Multistep syntheses/Retrosynthesis examples—for you to try as extra practice

Design a synthesis to make this polymer from 1,3-butadiene and benzene

Design a synthesis to make this polymer from benzene

199

1. According to Le Chatelier's principle, which reaction is favored, Fischer esterification, hydrolysis, or neither, when we:

Practice

A. use Dean-Stark trap and molecular sieves to remove water for the mixture.
Reaction favored is: _____
B. add more acid catalyst.
Reaction favored is: _____
C. add water.
Reaction favored is: _____
D. add methanol.
Reaction favored is: _____

2. Consider the two polymers and the three monomers shown. Which monomers would make each condensation polymer?

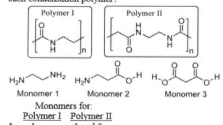

	Monomers for:	
---	Polymer I	Polymer II
A.	1	1 and 2
B.	1 and 2	2 and 3
C.	1 and 3	2
D.	2	3
E.	2	1 and 3

3. Which of the following alcohols can be formed from a reaction between an ester and a Grignard reagent (RMgX) in excess?

A.　　B.　　C.　　D.

E. none of the above alcohols can be formed from ester and Grignard

200

Practice

4. Add the mechanism arrows and all missing formal charges to this series of elementary steps. Note: HA and A⁻ signify an acid and a base, respectively.

How *many* missing formal charges and mechanism arrows were required to complete the mechanism?

	Missing formal charges	Mechanism arrows
A.	2	8
B.	2	6
C.	3	8
D.	3	7
E.	3	6

201

Enols and enolates

Acidity of α H

Keto and enol tautomers

Reactions via enol and enolates

Enolates of β–dicarbonyls

Enolate as nucleophile

Aldol

Claisen

Acetoacetic ester synthesis (make methyl ketones)

Malonic ester synthesis (make substituted acetic acids)

202

RXNs at the α-carbon of carbonyl compounds (enols and enolates)

Compare to recent reactions

Aldehydes and ketones

Carboxylic acid derivatives

(+ LG)

New: due to the weak acidity of hydrogen on carbon adjacent to the C=O (aka α-hydrogens), they can be deprotonated by strong base

RXNs at the α-carbon of carbonyl compounds (enols and enolates)

New: due to the weak acidity of hydrogen on carbon adjacent to the C=O (aka α-hydrogens), they can be deprotonated by strong base

enolate is resonance stabilized--it is the conjugate base of the reactant. pKa of reactant ~19-20--lower than expected

Laura Lanni

REVIEW: Recall enol form of ketone (orgo 1 alkyne hydrations)

Keto-enol tautomers are constitutional isomers.

The interconversion (in an equilibrium) is called tautomerization.

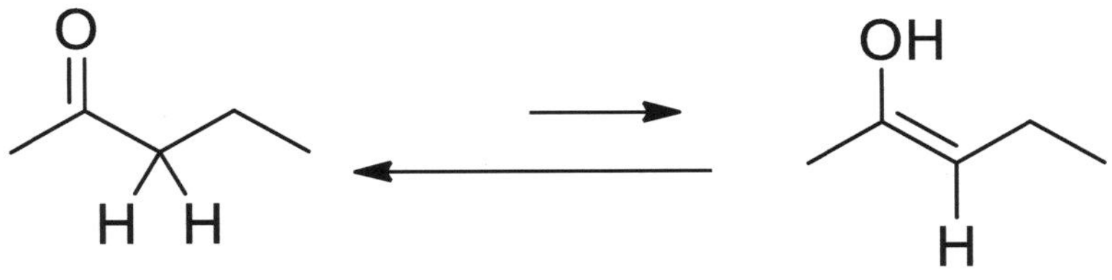

These are tautomers. They are in equilibrium and the ketone is favored. (NOT resonance)

205

Conjugate bases of the tautomers

Draw the conjugate base of each tautomer. (what is the relationship between the two conjugate bases?)

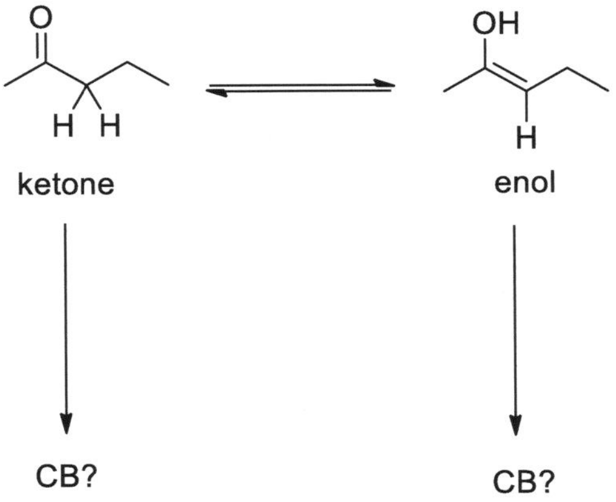

206

Special tautomer situation—β-dicarbonyls

Another special tautomer situation

Why does cyclohexa-2,4-diene-1-one exist ~100% in enol form?
(hint: Draw it. Draw its tautomer and then think.)

Laura Lanni

Enolization can be promoted (enhanced) with base (or acid)

Example with 3-methylbutanone and hydroxide (mechanism)

209

Acid-catalyzed Enolization

Example (and mech) with 3-methylbutanone

210

Enolization of a ketone with a chiral center α to carbonyl

Produces a **racemic mix** of ketone products. (Called racemization.)

example

Halogenation at the α-carbon

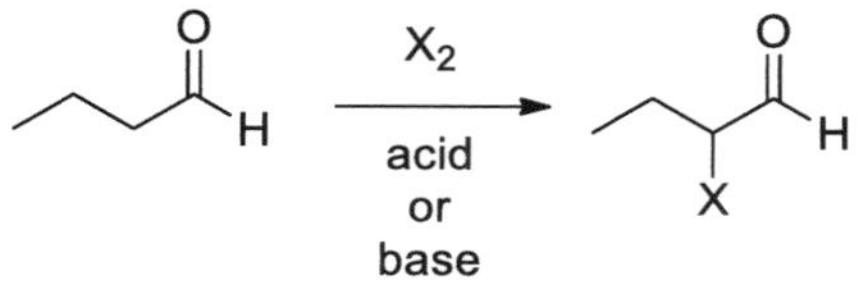

BASE PROMOTED is a 2-step reaction like this
  1. slow deprotonation
  2. fast α-halogenation

Mechanism and example

ACID-catalyzed halogenation (4 steps) (example and mechanism)

Base-catalyzed halogenation of methyl ketone at the α-carbon:
Haloform reaction (needs excess halogen and excess base)

Methyl ketone → multiple halogenations → carboxylate + haloform (HCX$_3$)

(The carboxylate product is the conjugate base of a carboxylic acid. Acid work up makes the COOH.)

mechanism

Base-catalyzed halogenation of methyl ketone at the α-carbon: Haloform reaction (notes)

The haloform reaction is a synthetic step that turns a methyl ketone into a carboxylic acid

If chloroform (HCCl$_3$) or bromoform (HCBr$_3$) are produced, they are liquids that can be extracted with organic solvents while the carboxylate remains in the aqueous phase (prior to acid workup).

If iodoform (HCI$_3$) is produced, it is a solid which will precipitate out and can be filtered off.

Base choice for deprotonation of α-hydrogen
(enolate formation)

must be strong

NaOEt is not strong enough. Look at equilibrium and pK$_a$s:

Need a base with **what pK$_a$ range for its conjugate acid (CA)**?_____

LDA

Lithium diisopropyl amide

Structure

Conjugate acid

Conjugate acid pKa? _____

Deprotonation of alpha (α) proton

makes a carbon nucleophile (enolate)!

(S_N2 on alkyl halide)

But first, a complication...

217

Complication: 2 different α-hydrogen(s)

(Regiochemistry of α-deprotonation—can be controlled by base choice)

Unsymmetrical ketone like butanone

218

Examples with nucleophilic enolate (S$_N$2 on alkyl halide (RX) electrophile)

(works best with 1° RX or benzylic-X to avoid elimination/promote substitution)

A way to make longer/more branched alkylated ketones or aldehydes

1. LDA

2. Methyl iodide
   (aka iodomethane)

1. LDA

2. Benzylbromide

Condensation and conjugate additions of C=O compounds

Claisen Condensation

Acylation of enolates

Aldol

Crossed **Aldol**

Cyclization via **Aldol**

Michael addition

Robinson annulation

Overview and definitions

1. <u>Condensation reactions</u> of carbonyls: the enol or enolate of one molecule reacts with C=O of another. A small molecule (like water or alcohol) condenses (is removed).

a. **Claisen condensation**: reaction of esters.

   (product β–ketoester)

b. **Aldol addition** and condensation: reaction of aldehydes / ketones.

   (product α,β-unsaturated carbonyl)

2. Conjugate additions: reaction of α,β-unsaturated carbonyl

221

Claisen Condensation: details, mechanism, examples

Make β-ketoesters from esters

mechanism

222

Claisen Condensation: details, mechanism, examples

Make β-ketoester from ester(s)

β-ketoester ion is so critical to this reaction. Esters with only 1 α H will not undergo Claisen. NEED that 2nd α H.

Examples:

Special Claisens—

       intramolecular (Dieckmann, cyclic)

       Crossed Claisen. Examples of each.

Blank pages for examples of Claisen

Blank pages for examples of Claisen

Practice

1. NaOPr
2. acid workup

A   B   C   D

practice

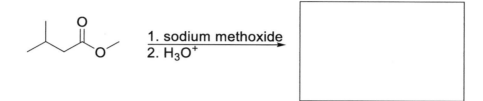

1. sodium methoxide
2. H_3O^+

Dieckmann Condensation

Cyclic Claisen: Useful for preparation of cyclic β-ketoesters

Example:

Diethyl ester of adipic acid reacts with

1.   sodium ethoxide followed by

2. hydronium neutralization.

     What is produced?

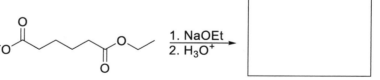

1. NaOEt
2. H_3O^+

More Dieckmann Condensation

Cyclic Claisen: Useful for preparation of cyclic β-ketoesters

Another one. Start with dimethyl ester of pimelic acid (7C diacid).

1. NaOMe
2. H_3O^+

Another with alkyl substituents...?

1. NaOEt
2. H_3O^+

(Go back and hydrolyze/decarboxylate each)

229

Crossed Claisen

Uses two different esters—one with NO α-Hs (it is the electrophile)

Examples of esters with no α-Hs:

Example of Crossed Claisen with ethyl acetate and ethyl benzoate

+

nucleophile   electrophile

1. NaOEt
2. H_3O^+

Another...

+

1. NaOEt
2. H_3O^+

(Later--go back and hydrolyze/decarboxylate each β-ketoester for practice)

230

After Claisen

What if there are two more steps on the β-ketoester Claisen products:

hydrolysis of the ester and decarboxylation?

231

Commercial break/review

What if the desired product is 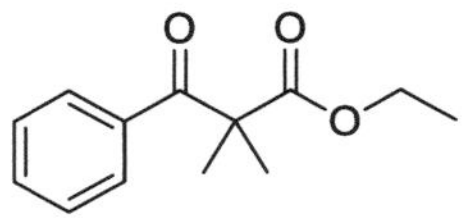 ??

Acylate the enolate!

(or just alkylate like acetoacetic ester synthesis (coming soon))

232

Crossed Claisen where both esters can be nucleophile or electrophile (makes a mix of products)— be able to predict all the products

What are all the possible **β-ketoester products** if we reacted two esters that *both* have 2 αH?

What are all the possible **ketone products** if we then hydrolyze and decarboxylate those β-ketoester products?

233

Crossed Claisen where both esters can be nucleophile or electrophile (makes a mix of products)— be able to predict all the products

Another example or work one in recitation?

234

Claisen RETROSYNTHESIS
Two examples

Design a synthesis to make each *via* Claisen (or Dieckmann):

1.

2.

PRACTICE

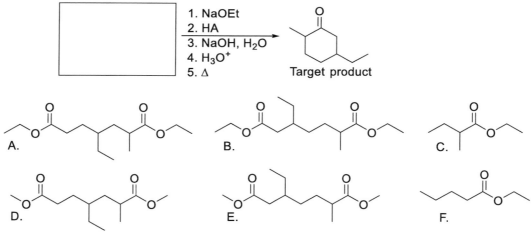

1. NaOEt
2. HA
3. NaOH, H₂O
4. H₃O⁺
5. Δ

Target product

A.   B.   C.

D.   E.   F.

G. A crossed reaction with two of these.   H. None of these

Laura Lanni

Aldol addition and condensation

Starts with aldehyde or ketone. Addition product is ALDOL

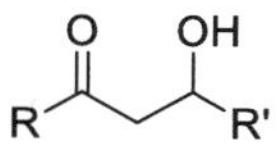

Further reaction with STRONG acid (OR BASE) (dehydration) gives
aldol condensation product:

α,β-unsaturated carbonyl

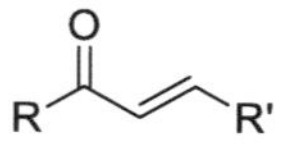

Examples and mechanism (next page).

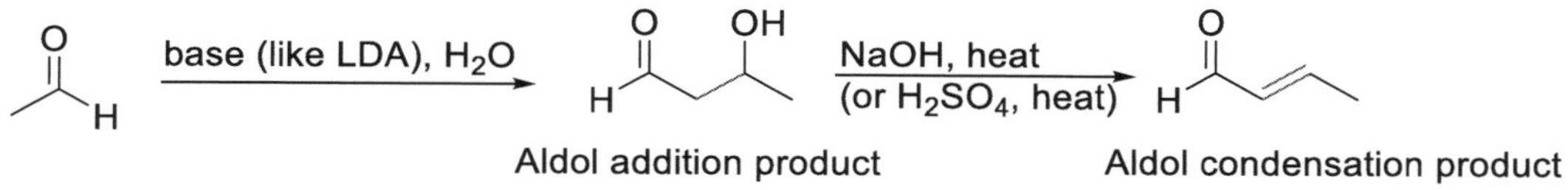

Aldol addition product   Aldol condensation product

237

Aldol mechanism

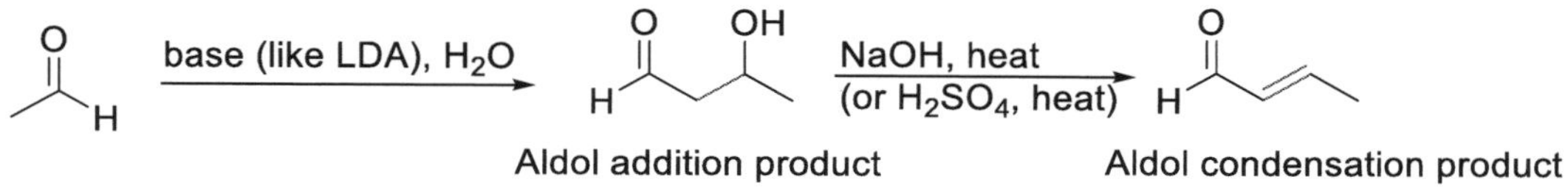

Aldol addition product   Aldol condensation product

238

Aldol examples

Predict product

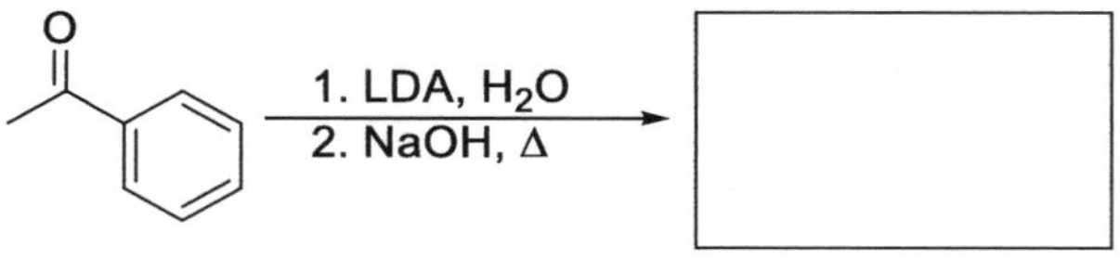

1. LDA, H₂O
2. NaOH, Δ

Predict reactant

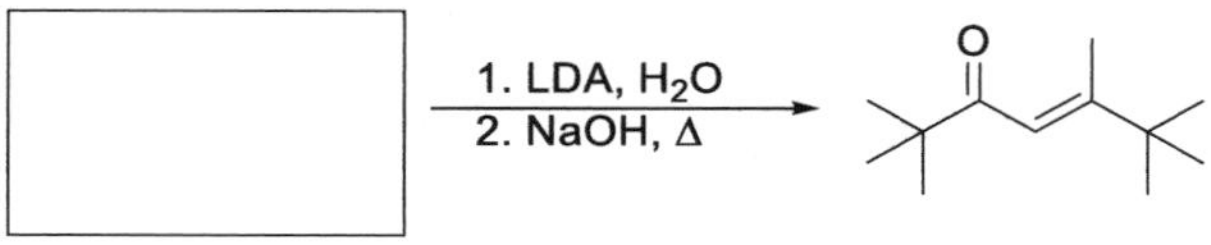

1. LDA, H₂O
2. NaOH, Δ

239

Additional reactions (reductions) which are possible on Aldol products (continuing with Aldol products from recent example)

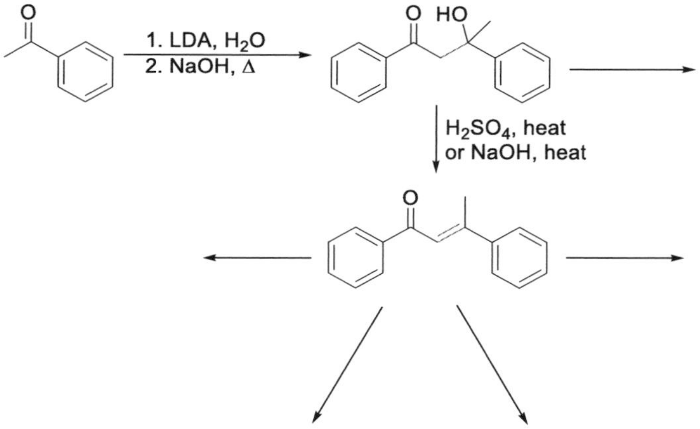

1. LDA, H₂O
2. NaOH, Δ

H₂SO₄, heat
or NaOH, heat

240

Crossed Aldol

Uses TWO different carbonyls

Example: ethanal and propanal (makes mixture of 4 products)

2 dimers (self-Aldol)

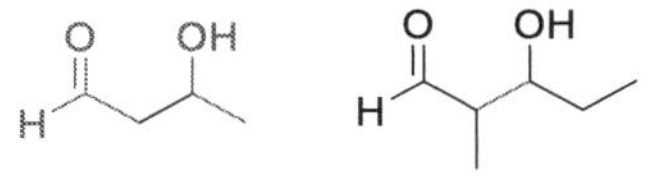

2 crossed products

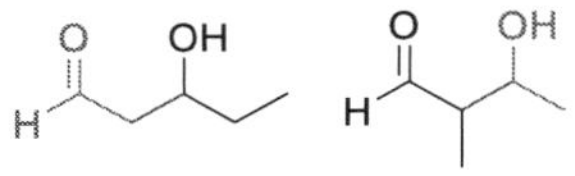

(Then make condensation products by dehydration with sodium hydroxide and heat...) 241

Crossed Aldol examples

More control of product when one starting material has NO α-hydrogens

Example: benzaldehyde and acetone

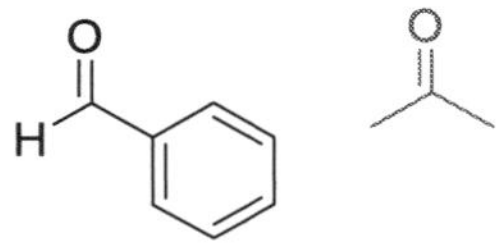

Example: formaldehyde and 2-methylpropanal

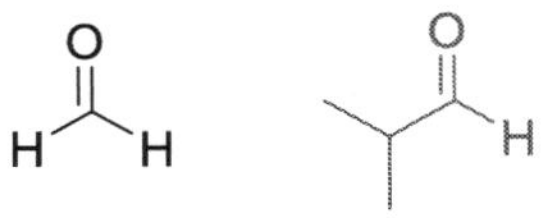

242

Directed Aldol—when both reactants have α-hydrogens

Use strong base (LDA) to PREFORM the desired (kinetic) enolate

Example (and what ifs?)

Desired product:

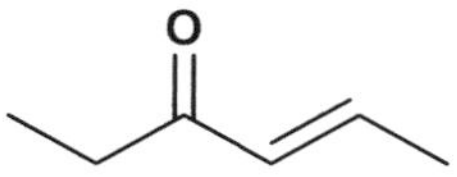

What if we changed order of addition?

What if we used WEAK base with original order of addition?

BE CAREFUL: strength of base AND order of addition matter

243

Aldol examples and RETROs

How would you make each *via* Aldol?

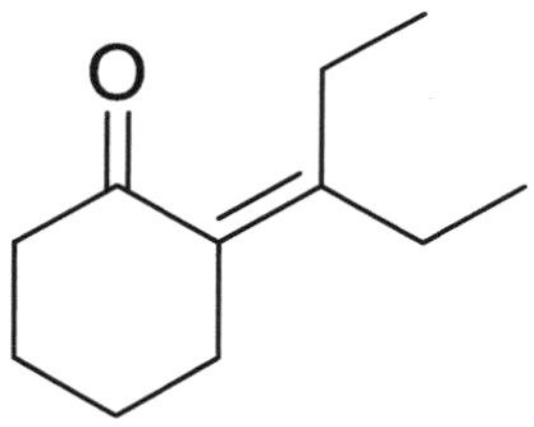

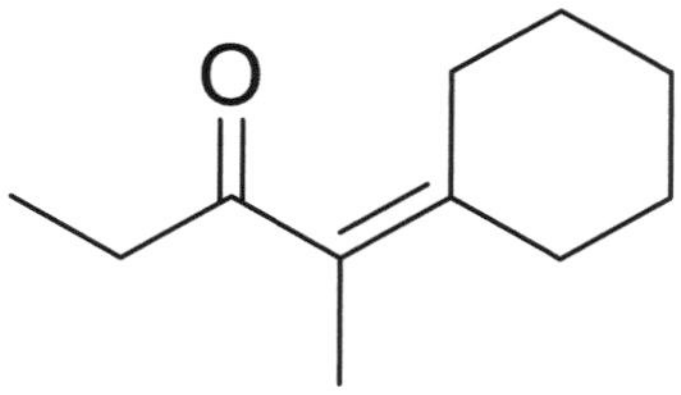

244

Cyclization *via* Aldol

$$\text{(structure)} \xrightarrow{\text{-OH}} \xrightarrow[\text{(or NaOH, heat)}]{H_2SO_4} \text{three products}$$

245

ORGANIC CHEMISTRY FUNCTIONAL GROUP INTERCONVERSIONS

Alkane

Alkene

Alkyne

Alcohol

Alkyl halide

Epoxide

Halohydrin

benzene

Aldehyde

Ketone

Carboxylic acid

Ester

Acid chloride

Anhydride

Amide

Acetal (ketal)

hemiacetal (hemiketal)

Imine

Enamine-

Amine

diacid

Beta-keto ester

Beta-keto acid

Aldol addition product

α,β-unsaturated carbonyl

246

Design two ways to convert ethyl bromide to propanoic acid.

Put the pieces together
Alkene to α,β-unsaturated carbonyl…

Start with alkene

Make alcohol (addition (hydration), ch 8, orgo 1)

Make carboxylic acid (oxidation)

Make ester (Fischer)

Ester makes β-ketoester (Claisen)

Hydrolysis makes β-ketoacid

Decarboxylation makes ketone

Make Aldol addition product

Dehydrate, makes α,β-unsaturated carbonyl

PRACTICE

1. Which is an inappropriate mechanistic step in conversion of 2-pentanone to the ketal as shown? (NOTE: all mechanism arrows shown are heterolytic.)

HA, 2 equiv ethanol

A.

B.

C.

D.

E. All are appropriate mechanistic steps.

2. Which series of reagents will complete each sequence of reactions in this multistep synthesis of isopropyl benzoate?

Sequence 1: benzene is converted to benzoic acid
Sequence 2: propene is converted to isopropanol
Sequence 3: benzoic acid and isopropanol are converted to isopropyl benzoate

isopropyl benzoate

	Sequence 1	Sequence 2	Sequence 3
A.	1. AlCl$_3$, [H-(C=O)-Cl] 2. H$_2$CrO$_4$	1. BH$_3$ 2. H$_2$O$_2$, NaOH	HA, H$_2$O
B.	1. AlCl$_3$, CH$_3$Cl 2. H$_2$CrO$_4$	1. H$_2$SO$_4$. H$_2$O	HA, remove H$_2$O
C.	1. AlCl$_3$, [H-(C=O)-Cl] 2. H$_2$CrO$_4$	1. BH$_3$ 2. H$_2$O$_2$, NaOH	HA, remove H$_2$O
D.	1. AlCl$_3$, CH$_3$Cl 2. H$_2$CrO$_4$	1. H$_2$SO$_4$, H$_2$O	HA, H$_2$O

E. None of these will produce the target ester.

PRACTICE

3. Which is the missing reactant before this series of steps?

| ? | 1. HBr,ROOR 2. NaCN 3. H$_3$O$^+$, heat 4. SOCl$_2$ 5. (Et)$_2$CuLi 6. NaBH$_4$, MeOH | → 3-hexanol |

A. 2-butene   D. ethene
B. 1-butene   E. 1-pentene
C. propene

4. Which would be *least likely to form* after this series of reactions?

1. NaOEt
2. HA (aq)
3. heat

?

A.

D. All will form in equal amounts.

B.

E. None of these will form.

C.

Acetoacetic ester and malonic ester reactions (and sequence)

251

Examples with nucleophilic enolate (S_N2 on alkyl halide (RX) electrophile)
(works best with 1° RX or benzylic-X to avoid elimination/promote substitution)

A way to make longer/more branched alkylated ketones or aldehydes

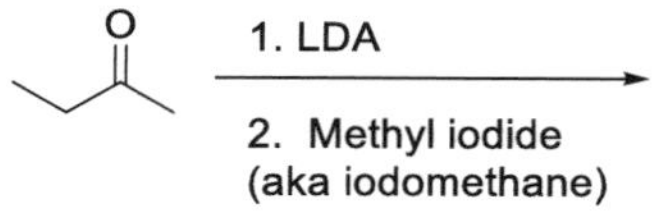

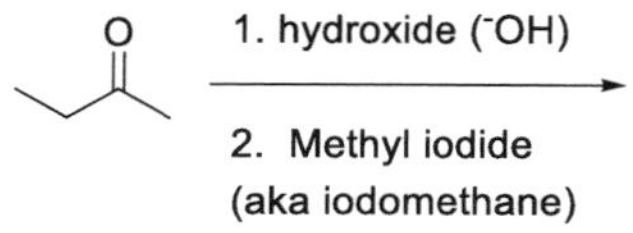

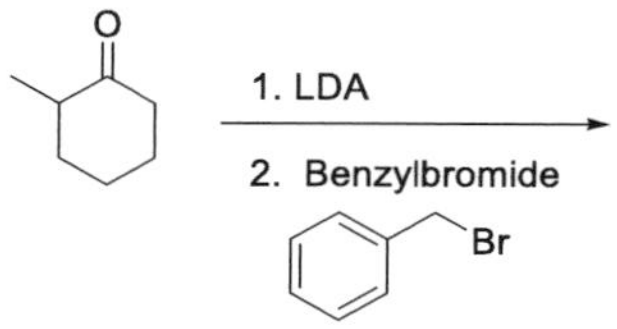

1. LDA

2. Methyl iodide
(aka iodomethane)

1. hydroxide (⁻OH)

2. Methyl iodide
(aka iodomethane)

1. LDA

2. Benzylbromide

252

Also works with αH on esters

Example: ethyl butanoate/LDA/1-iodopropane

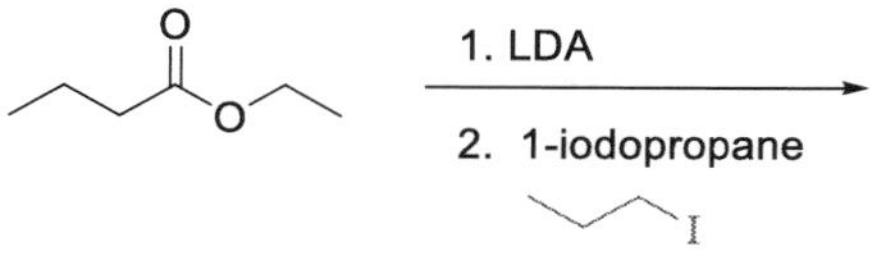

1. LDA
2. 1-iodopropane

Another example with cyclic ester

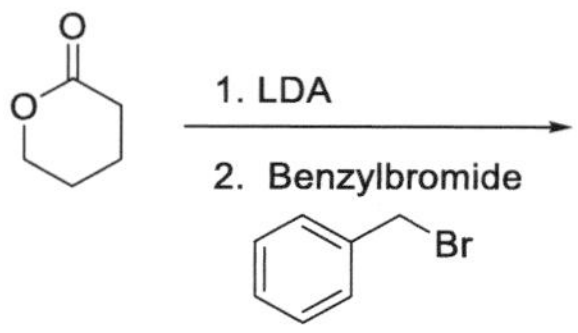

1. LDA
2. Benzylbromide

Another:

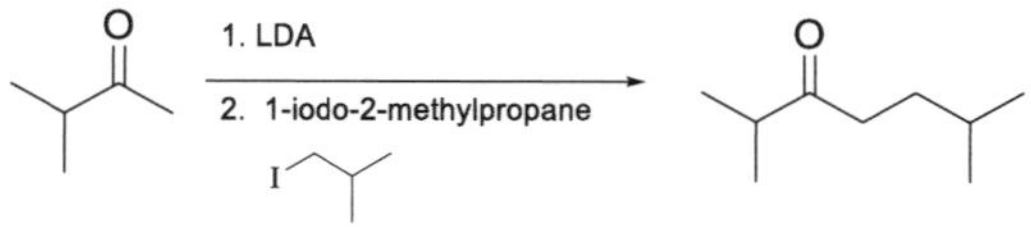

1. LDA
2. 1-iodo-2-methylpropane

α-alkylation works with β–dicarbonyl compounds
(but with weak base. Why? pKa, resonance stabilized enolate)

pK_a and resonance considerations

2 different –dicarbonyl compounds are used a lot:

Acetoacetic ester

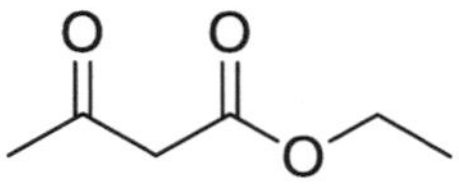

Malonic ester (diethylmalonate)

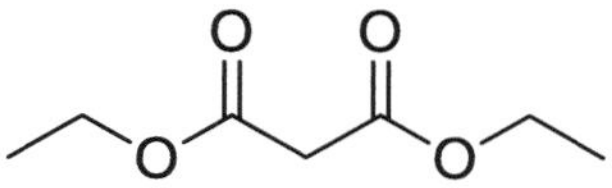

Acetoacetic ester synthesis

Used to synthesize methyl ketones

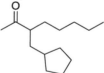

(deprotonation) (S_N2) new bond

But wait. THAT's not a methyl ketone...

Can be repeated.

Then hydrolyze the ester.

Then decarboxylate the β-keto acid...to make final product:

(know all mechanisms)

a methyl ketone

255

Acetoacetic ester synthesis: RETRO synthesis

Write a retrosynthesis and design a series of synthetic steps to make this methyl ketone
using **acetoacetic ester synthesis**
followed by ester **hydrolysis** and **decarboxylation**.

256

Acetoacetic ester

Try one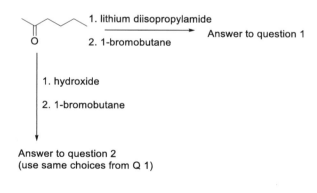

What if the final product is reacted with

1. excess hydroxide and bromine, and then 2. acid workup?

257

Practice

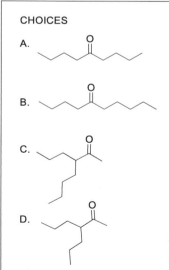

1. lithium diisopropylamide

2. 1-bromobutane → Answer to question 1

1. hydroxide

2. 1-bromobutane

Answer to question 2
(use same choices from Q 1)

CHOICES

A.

B.

C.

D.

258

Acetoacetic ester can also be used...

...as nucleophile to attach acid chloride electrophiles in a process called ACYLATION

Subsequent hydrolysis and decarboxylation yields β-dicarbonyl

259

Next: diethylmalonate (aka malonic ester)

Diethylmalonate is the diethyl ester of malonic acid
(Recall commercial: OMSGA)

Following the same steps as acetoacetic ester synthesis, then hydrolysis and decarboxylation, produces **substituted acetic acids.**

1. NaO⌐
2. ⌐I
3. NaO⌐
4. ⌐I

Let's go through each step to
show how this product is made.

5. NaOH
6. H_3O^+
7. heat

260

Next: diethylmalonate (aka malonic ester)

Step-wise analysis with some mechanism

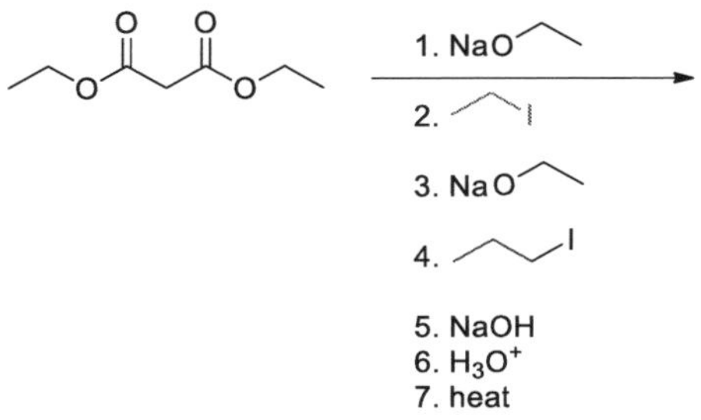

1. NaO⌒
2. ⌒I
3. NaO⌒
4. ⌒⌒I
5. NaOH
6. H_3O^+
7. heat

261

Diethylmalonate FAQ

After hydrolysis there are TWO COOH groups

In decarboxylation, why is only ONE COOH removed?

(mechanism of *decarboxylation of β-diacid* gives the answer)

262

Diethylmalonate: TWO interesting examples

with dihaloalkanes

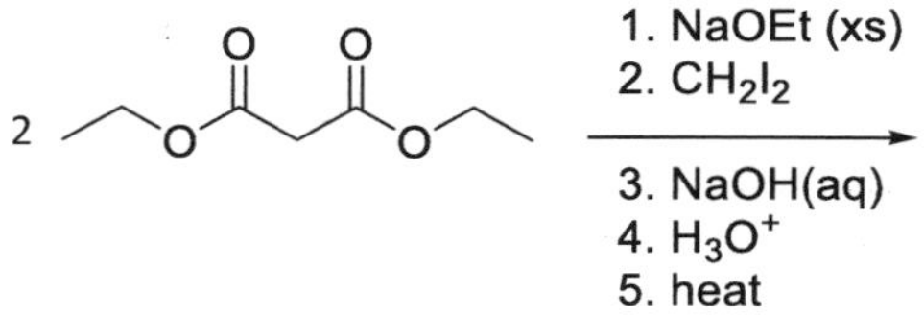

2 [diethyl malonate structure]

1. NaOEt (xs)
2. CH_2I_2
———————→
3. NaOH(aq)
4. H_3O^+
5. heat

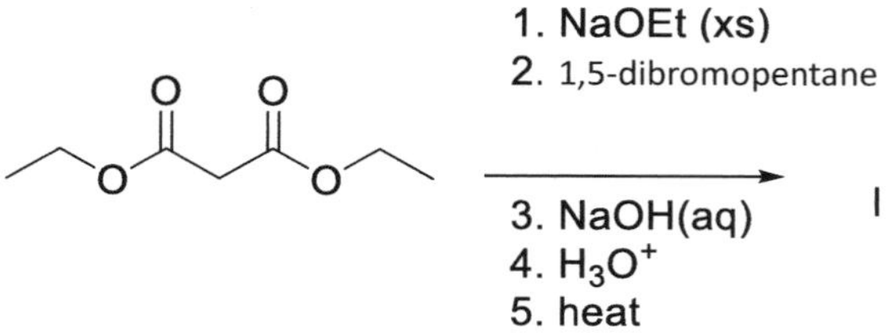

[diethyl malonate structure]

1. NaOEt (xs)
2. 1,5-dibromopentane
———————→
3. NaOH(aq)   I
4. H_3O^+
5. heat

263

RECAP

Use acetoacetic ester synthesis to make methyl ketones from

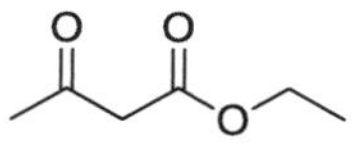

Use malonic ester synthesis to make carboxylic acids from

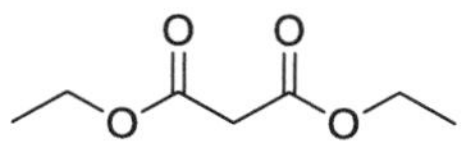

A few more examples.

264

More practice—for you to try

design a retrosynthesis and a series of synthetic steps

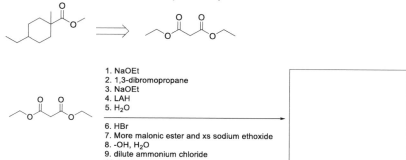

1. NaOEt
2. 1,3-dibromopropane
3. NaOEt
4. LAH
5. H_2O

6. HBr
7. More malonic ester and xs sodium ethoxide
8. -OH, H_2O
9. dilute ammonium chloride
10. heat

propose a mechanism for this reaction

MeOH, H_2SO_4

265

A few more examples for you to try

pentanoic acid

266

Additions to α,β-unsaturated aldehydes and ketones

2 possible ways

1. Addition across C=O, called simple addition ("1,2-addition" "direct addition")

    With nucleophiles like Grignard

2. Addition of NUCleophile to carbon #4 and H to oxygen, called conjugate addition ("1,4-addition") (involves tautomerization)

    With nucleophiles like Gilman or enolate

Consideration: strong vs weak nucleophiles...

267

Conjugate addition

Consider resonance structures

268

Conjugate addition of enolate as nucleophile

Michael addition (1887 Arthur Michael)

Enolate + α,β-unsaturated carbonyl → 1,5-dicarbonyl

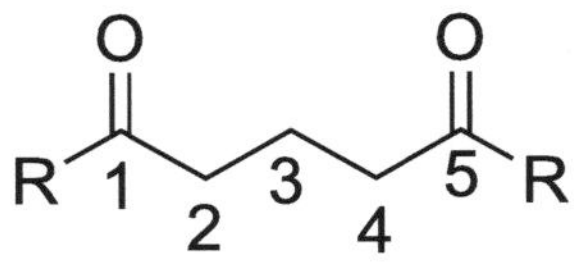

Examples and mechanism

269

RETRO examples
How would you make...?

270

Multistep syntheses

Robinson Annulation (ring formation)

A Michael addition of a cyclic β–dicarbonyl to α,β–unsaturated carbonyl followed by Aldol condensation—result: builds one ring onto another.

Example

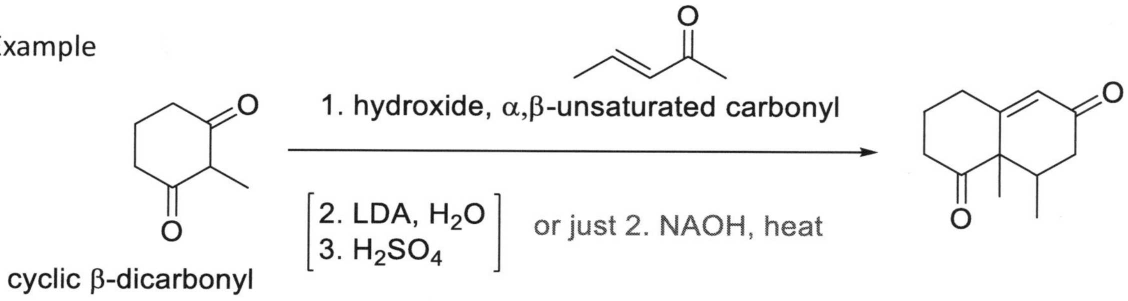

1. hydroxide, α,β-unsaturated carbonyl

$\begin{bmatrix} 2.\ LDA,\ H_2O \\ 3.\ H_2SO_4 \end{bmatrix}$ or just 2. NAOH, heat

cyclic β-dicarbonyl

Enolate recap

BASICS (tautomers, resonance, conjugate acid and base pairs)

Enolate as nucleophile with RX (S_N2), base choice (pKa) (with various enolates)

Haloform reaction

Racemization (chiral αC)

β-dicarbonyls: Acetoacetic ester and malonic ester syntheses (both may be followed by hydrolysis and decarboxylation)

Claisen (self) (may be followed by hydrolysis and decarboxylation)

Crossed Claisen (mess)

Cyclic Claisen (Dieckmann)

Aldol (self)/dehydration

Crossed Aldol

Directed Aldol

Cyclic Aldol

Reductions (review) on Aldol products

Michael addition (conjugate addition)

273

Reaction Review from orgo 1 and orgo 2

274

Functional groups
Alkane
Alkene
Alkyne
Alcohol
Alkyl halide
Epoxide
Halohydrin
benzene
Aldehyde
Ketone
Carboxylic acid
Ester
Acid chloride
Anhydride
Amide
Acetal (ketal)
hemiacetal (hemiketal)
Imine
Enamine
Amine
diacid
Beta-keto ester
Beta-keto acid
Beta-diacid

Getting ready for comprehensive year-long organic final exam
understand and apply the how and why, instead of memorizing a million unconnected "facts"

Orgo 1 Topics

Cyclohexane chairs, boats, cis, trans, axial, equatorial

Fischer projections, Newman projections

Stereochemistry, R, S, enantiomers, diastereomers, meso, achiral, chiral

Additions to alkenes, alkynes, extending alkynes

Radical reactions

Resonance

SO many ways to halogenate

Alkanes

Alkenes

Alkynes

Allylic, benzylic

Butadiene—1,2 vs 1,4,
        kinetic vs thermodynamic control

Markovnikov, anti-Markovnikov

Vicinal, geminal dihalide

Tetrahalogen

EAS halogenation

Mechanisms

Elementary steps: proton transfer, nuc attack, LG leaves, concerted, carbocation formation, carbocation rearrangement...slow vs fast, E_a, reaction coord diagram, kinetics, rate law...

Heterolytic and homolytic arrows

Nucleophiles and electrophiles

Formal charges

275

Laura Lanni

Made in the USA
Columbia, SC
07 January 2022